Boys and Girls Together

in K–6 Classrooms

SMALL BOOK SERIES
#5
SMALL BOOK SERIES

Tamara Grogan

All net proceeds from the sale of *Boys and Girls Together: Improving Gender Relationships in K–6 Classrooms* support the work of Northeast Foundation for Children, a nonprofit educational organization whose mission is to foster safe, challenging, and joyful classrooms and schools, K–8.

ISBN 1-892989-12-3
Library of Congress catalog card number 2003111435

First printing November 2003

Photographs: Peter Wrenn, Cherry Wyman

Cover and book design: Woodward Design

Northeast Foundation for Children
39 Montague City Road
Greenfield, MA 01301
1-800-360-6332
www.responsiveclassroom.org

Table of Contents

Acknowledgments

THERE ARE MANY PEOPLE whose work and support have helped bring this book into the world. I wish to thank:

Lynn Bechtel, editor and writer at Northeast Foundation for Children (NEFC), first and most fervently, for taking on the project soon after joining the NEFC publications staff. In the midst of all her other new responsibilities, she gave the book shape, clarity, organization, and cohesiveness. Lynn's additional research and writing also added value to the book. The book would not exist without the enormous amount of work she devoted to it.

Mary Beth Forton, NEFC director of publications, for her constant encouragement and helpful conversation while we toiled up long hills on bicycles and talked around the editorial staff table back in the office.

Roxann Kriete, NEFC executive director, for her interest in the project from the very beginning and her pragmatic suggestions for getting it underway and moving it along.

Sharon Dunn, longtime NEFC board member, for her interest in documenting what had been done over the years to promote gender equity and awareness at the Greenfield Center School. Her curiosity was the spark that set the idea burning for the rest of us.

Ruth Sidney Charney, Bob Fricker, Chip Wood, Alice Yang, and Marianne Millette-Kelly for their careful reading of the manuscript; their insightful comments; and the ideas, suggestions, and examples they contributed.

Jeff and Leslie Woodward, graphic designers, for their attention to detail, their patience with an ever-changing timeline, and as always, their beautiful book design.

Janice Gadaire Fleuriel, copy editor and proofreader, for her sharp eye, her interest in the project, and her thoughtful comments and suggestions.

Finally, I wish to thank every educator mentioned in these pages—a long list—whose ideas and stories are the fundamental basis for the book. Thank you for sharing your time and expertise with me. Thank you for your humor and insight. Talking to you was the best part of all.

This book is dedicated to Tess and her friends—the girls and the boys.

Introduction
Girls on One Side, Boys on the Other

I T'S EARLY OCTOBER *and life has settled into a comfortable routine in Ms. James's third grade classroom. Rules and behavior expectations have been established, a sense of community is growing, and students seem invested in their academic work.*

Ms. James is beginning to grow uneasy, however, about the separation and tension she observes between boys and girls. For example, as students gathered today for their morning gathering, Ms. James noticed that once again all the boys clustered on one side of the meeting circle and all the girls on the other. The same thing happened during choice time, when girls and boys gathered in separate work groups. Yesterday, Tyrone and Steven announced that they wanted to join Shameka and Marie on a geology project but Marie said, indignantly, "No way. We don't want to work with boys. You'll just mess everything up."

And whenever Ms. James is on lunchroom duty, she sees that the girls gravitate to one table and the boys to another. One day she was delighted to see Joey, who is usually fairly shy, approach Janet at the girls' table. But the situation quickly turned nasty when Alex began taunting him, "Joey's got a girlfriend, Joey's got a girlfriend," and the girls started giggling.

Scenes such as these are common in elementary schools: boys or girls left out for being the wrong gender; talents, ideas, and enthusiasm rejected because someone belongs to the other sex; girls and boys teasing and taunting each other as they defend their positions on either side of the gender divide.

Drawing the gender line

For a variety of cultural, biological, and social reasons, children in large groups tend to self-segregate along gender lines. Research even documents the existence of "gender enforcers," students like Alex in the opening scenario who "snap into action whenever another child attempts to violate a gender boundary." (Szegedy-Maszak 2001, 58)

But while children may enforce this line drawn in the sand, it's important to note that they didn't create it. American society sorts itself along gender lines from the first moments of a child's life when it's clearly established that blue is for boys and pink for girls. Throughout a child's early years, parents make many choices regarding clothing, toys, books, and activities based on subtle and not-so-subtle gender distinctions. And in school, the differentiation often gets reinforced when children are regularly divided into groupings based on gender.

Although we've come a long way from the days of elementary schools with enforced separate building entrances for boys and girls, gender is still regularly used to sort students: "boys on this side, girls on the other" is a quick, efficient way to line students up or make teams. Barrie Thorne, sociologist and author of *Gender Play: Boys and Girls in School,* notes:

Teachers use [gender] to mark out groups, usually for social control. . . .

By frequently using gender labels when they interact with kids, adults make being a boy or girl central to self-definition and to the ongoing life of schools. (Thorne 1993, 34–35)

Thorne notes that even as simple a statement as "Good morning, boys and girls" can serve to separate students by gender, increasing gender's visibility in school and making it seem important. (Thorne 1993, 35)

This emphasis on gender distinctions, coming at children from many different places in their lives, can negatively influence how girls and boys view one another. At its worst, it drives boys and girls apart, making friendship across gender lines difficult. The difficulty often intensifies at school where the crowded, public nature of the setting provides many witnesses to children's behavior and increases the likelihood of "gender enforcers" taking action. The risk of teasing at school, as Thorne notes, is high; it is a rare child who is heroic enough to do things differently from everyone else. (Thorne 1993, 53)

2

Kids will be kids?

As early as kindergarten and first grade, girls and boys will begin to self-segregate in school according to gender, most noticeably on the playground and in the lunchroom. But while teachers might notice early signs of the gender split in the primary grades, it becomes most pronounced, and often adversarial, in about the third grade. This is when boys and girls not only begin to separate by gender in school, but also stop inviting each other to come over after school and start having single-gender birthday parties. Rather than simply self-segregating, children in these grades begin to actively resist gender mixing. It's at this age that girls and boys will often complain about sitting or working together in the classroom and refuse to play together at recess.

Because this preference for same-gender friends and resistance to gender mixing is a predictable part of child development, it's tempting for busy teachers, administrators, and family members to dismiss problems between boys and girls with a simple, "Kids will be kids."

But the divide between boys and girls in school and the negative behaviors that frequently come with it are worth paying attention to. In fact, facing them head-on is a prerequisite to successful teaching in many classrooms, where teachers are confronted daily with taunting, excluding, mocking, name-calling, and hurtful notes and drawings, by both girls and boys.

All of this interferes with attempts to build community, prevents boys and girls from working successfully together, undermines the academic agenda, and creates an unsafe learning environment. As veteran teacher Ruth Sidney Charney remarks:

> Sorting by gender works against what we most want: to be fulfilled and to build a community. If boys are always here, girls always there, it divides the community. It's our job to help children reach their potential, which often means we have to unsort the sorted.

Teachers can make a difference

While it can sometimes feel like swimming against a powerful tide, teachers do have the power to change things, at least in their own classrooms. Teachers have unique opportunities every day, in all the choices they make, to build each gender's knowledge of and respect for the other, and to create opportunities for girls and boys to work and play together harmoniously. These experiences can create impressions that will follow students for the rest of their lives.

Even the small daily decisions a teacher makes, such as how to have students line up, how to group students for work projects, or how to arrange the seating chart, have the potential to powerfully affect the relationships between boys and girls at school. Consider the following glimpse of Ms. James's classroom after she has spent several months working to bridge the gender gap:

It's the first day back at school after the February break. As the students come together for their morning gathering, they split into all-girl and all-boy clumps. Ms. James points to the meeting rules that are posted on the wall. "Who remembers how we're supposed to sit at meeting?" she asks. "Boy/girl," Robert says, and quickly the students rearrange themselves. A few students frown and grumble as they leave their best friends but soon they're engaged in lively conversations with other students sitting near them.

Later, when students break into pairs to work on a writing project, Ms. James is pleased to see that the students choose work partners based on shared interests and abilities and that there are many girl/boy pairings. It really does seem as though boys and girls have learned how to get along: not as best friends but certainly as responsible and friendly work partners and classmates.

In the lunchroom, girls and boys still gravitate toward separate tables. Ms. James watches with concern one day as Olin approaches a table of all girls. Ms. James knows that this is a situation ripe for teasing and taunting. But she relaxes when Leslie greets Olin with a straightforward, "Hey Olin. What's up?" and the rest of the students simply continue eating and talking.

"But I want to be with my friends!"

Working to "unsort the sorted" doesn't mean that boys should never work only with boys or girls only with girls. Nor does it mean that teachers should discourage same-gender friendships or social groupings at school. No one can deny the value of same-gender friendships. People who are "like you" are powerfully attractive; once children learn that they share a category with others, they want to understand what the category means: What *is* a girl? What *is* a boy? They derive many clues about self-identity from same-gender peers.

Same-gender friendships also feel safe to young children while providing them with opportunities to explore differences beyond gender and to decide what they like in a person. Over the past few years, I have enjoyed hearing my daughter's developing rationale for liking her best friend. When they were in kindergarten, it was "I just like her." As time passed, her reasons became more sophisticated: "She is peaceful." "She is good at math." "She is wise. She would make a good president of the United States." Same-gender friendships also become increasingly important during puberty, when gender becomes a much more insistent force, and girls and boys look to their same-gender peers for information and support.

But while the desire to be with same-gender friends is a natural one, it can also undermine the teacher's desire to build a strong classroom community. When boys are *always* over here and girls *always* over there, the sense of community is fractured. Fortunately, there are many things a teacher can do to counter this trend and bring boys and girls together in school in positive ways. Within every school day there are countless opportunities for boys and girls to learn to work and play together in a friendly, respectful manner, outside the box of gender or cliques or favorite friend status. This book offers a starting point.

Unsorting the sorted

The goal of this book is to give elementary school teachers practical strategies for positively influencing how boys and girls relate to one another at school. Ten strategies are offered, which will help teachers begin to "unsort the sorted" by:

- Fostering caring bonds and friendships between girls and boys, based on shared interests, respect, and empathy
- Encouraging children to share interests and ideas with a wide range of classmates, regardless of gender
- Helping children take part in a rich variety of activities, regardless of gender

Many elementary school teachers were interviewed for this book. They shared their challenges as well as their successes and the specific strategies that have worked best for encouraging positive relationships between boys and girls at school. The strategies generally fall into the following areas, reflected in the organization of the book:

- Teacher Awareness
- Classroom Management
- The Curriculum
- Outside the Classroom (recess and lunch)

Be a patient gardener

Every teacher interviewed for this book expressed a belief in the strength of accumulated experience, that children learn how to relate to one another over the course of many years and with many opportunities to practice, make mistakes, and try again. All agree, too, that the task seems overwhelming at times. Jay Lord, long-time teacher and cofounder of Northeast Foundation for Children, notes, "Gender issues are not something you can break down and solve in five minutes."

But like the other teachers interviewed, Lord feels positive that change can occur, over time, in increments. Teachers, luckily, have a full repertoire of possible influences. Even more importantly, they have time on their side. By junior high, students will have spent over 7,000 hours with teachers! (Horgan 1995, 45) This is as much or more time than most have spent with their parents, and enough time to make a difference.

Teachers scatter seeds in their classrooms knowing that some may not take root at all, while others may take years to reach the sunlight. Like other patient gardeners, teachers improve the quality of the soil and work a little every day. They celebrate small achievements. They recover from failure. They water their gardens, and wait, and hope.

Works Cited

Horgan, Dianne D. 1995. *Achieving Gender Equity: Strategies for the Classroom*. Boston, MA: Allyn and Bacon.

Szegedy-Maszak, Marianne. 2001. "The Power of Gender: Boys Will Be Boys." *U. S. News and World Report* (June 4): 52.

Thorne, Barrie. 1993. *Gender Play: Girls and Boys in School*. New Brunswick, NJ: Rutgers University Press.

Teacher Awareness:
The Starting Point

Strategy One:
Know Your Students

Strategy Two:
Know Yourself

FOR MANY PEOPLE, the first step towards change is assessment of the current situation: what's working well, what's not working well, what most needs adjusting. To foster caring, empathic relationships between students, regardless of gender, teachers need to find time for observation and reflection. But this can be difficult as the busy day moves by, filled with demands for a teacher's time and attention.

But assessment doesn't have to be a lengthy process. It can be as simple as taking a half-hour a day for several days to observe students, and then ten minutes after school to reflect on the observations. Points to consider might include:

• Who are my students, both culturally and developmentally?

• What do I believe about gender relationships?

• What do I do and say that fosters—or impedes—positive relationships between boys and girls?

The two strategies discussed in this section offer starting points for these assessments.

Strategy One: Know Your Students

I T'S EARLY FALL *in Ms. Duvall's sixth grade classroom, and the boys and girls eye each other warily. Over the summer, many of the girls turned the corner into early adolescence and are now sporting lipstick, eye shadow, and stylish haircuts and clothes. By comparison, many of the boys seem awkward and young. The gap between the two groups appears to be widening. However, there is a small group of two boys and two girls who hang out together whenever they have free time. At lunch they take over a table in the cafeteria, where they giggle, flirt, and whisper. Recently, Ms. Duvall has noticed that the group of four now seems more like two couples. She observes them holding hands and passing notes while the rest of the class grows increasingly uncomfortable with their behavior.*

In Mr. Stringfellow's K–1 classroom, boys and girls move happily around the room, working in the block area, the drama corner, and the art center. Mr. Stringfellow is pleased that boys and girls are working together and that no one is excluded from a particular area or group. But at the end of the third week of school, Mr. Stringfellow gets a phone call from Jeremy's father saying that Jeremy told him he'd spent part of the morning playing dress-up with a group of girls. Mr. Stringfellow explains that the group was acting out a scene from a book that the class is reading together. But Jeremy's father is adamant: he doesn't want his son "wasting his time in school playing girls' games." Mr. Stringfellow responds by saying that the drama corner isn't only for girls—all students get a chance to work there. He invites Jeremy's father to come in for a conversation about the curriculum and to see the classroom setup.

Ms. Logan has worked hard to structure recess so that everyone in her fourth grade class has a chance to participate and have fun. There's always an active game, such as "Silly Soccer," which the children love to play (for a full description, see Strategy Ten). But Ms. Logan makes sure there are other activities available, some quiet and some more active. During family night, Julia's grand-mother takes Ms. Logan aside and says that she's concerned about Julia playing rough games with boys. Ms. Logan listens carefully to her concerns. She assures Julia's grandmother that she monitors games carefully to make sure everyone stays safe and comfortable. And she also lets the grandmother know that there are always several activity choices at recess.

As the above examples illustrate, several factors influence how boys and girls relate to one another in school. Developmental stages, as well as family and community values, all have an impact on students' willingness to step across the gender gap. Assumptions that teachers might make about the importance of—or even what constitutes—positive gender relationships may not hold true for students or their families. Teachers who are committed to improving gender relationships in school will want to:

- Get to know the students—individually, culturally, and developmentally

- Get to know the families

This knowledge will help teachers plan more effectively and better understand any resistance or discomfort they might encounter along the way.

Pay attention to developmental stage

All children go through predictable developmental stages, and at some of these stages, the inclination is to seek out same-gender social groupings. Being aware of this tendency can help you know how, when, and to what extent you want to implement strategies for building positive relationships between boys and girls. Below, you will find information about the impact of development on children's willingness to work in mixed gender groups (adapted from *Yardsticks: Children in the Classroom Ages 4–14, A Resource for Parents and Teachers* by Chip Wood). As you consider this information, please keep these two points about child development in mind:

- Chronological age does not always match developmental age.

A statement such as "eight-year-olds don't like to take risks" might apply to many children who are chronologically eight, but

12

not to all. It addresses a developmental trend but is not an absolute rule. Children's growth and development follow reasonably predictable patterns, but growth is deeply influenced by culture, personality, and environment. While children may go through predictable stages in a predictable order, not all children will go through the stages at the same rate.

• Individual development is uneven.

A child might mature quickly in one area, such as cognitive ability, but more slowly in another, such as social competence or physical ability.

Children ages four through seven

From ages four through seven, boys and girls are generally more willing to mix with each other than at older ages. There is less self-consciousness about boys playing with girls and girls with boys, and very young students may not yet have made a clear distinction between male and female.

But these are also years of rapid and dramatic change. At age four, many children are just beginning to move away from parallel play, but by six, many children develop a strong network of friends (including one "best friend," although the designated one may change frequently). The older children get, the more likely they are to reflect societal norms about gender. It's quite likely, for instance, that by ages six and seven boys and girls will start finding it harder to be friends with each other.

One mother tells the story of her six-year-old son whose closest friend since age four was a girl. The friend called one night, in considerable conflict. She wanted to invite the boy to her sixth birthday party but all the other guests were girls. What would they think about a boy attending the party? And how would he feel? "There will be ten girls there and you," she explained, "and we'll be doing lots of girl things like painting our fingernails and toenails." The boy assured her that this would be fine. He liked to paint his fingernails and toenails, too, he said. But the girl still worried. She finally decided that he could come to the party and she would get black nail polish for him, "a color that's better for boys," she said.

Since children at these early ages are still generally open to working and playing with a wide variety of classmates, these are good years for teachers to encourage frequent gender mixing and establish clear expectations for positive relationships between boys and girls. Creating classroom rules that emphasize respect and inclusion, and teaching and practicing social skills such as cooperation and empathy will help set the stage for positive relationships between boys and girls throughout their years in school.

Children ages eight through ten

By age eight, gender boundaries are more clearly drawn. As Wood notes, "Eight-year-olds tend to gravitate toward their own gender when making choices about working and playing with others. On the playground, the waves of boys chasing girls or girls chasing boys at recess are often eight-year-olds." (Wood 1997, 84)

Around age eight, boys and girls also begin to sort themselves according to competence. They want to do things they're good at and are reluctant to risk trying new things, particularly in areas where they doubt their skills. This often serves to further divide boys and girls.

Second-third grade combination teacher Terry Kayne says:

It amazes me how frequently the class ends up separating along boy-girl lines, especially in third grade. Sometimes it seems almost inconceivable to have third grade boys and girls work and play with each other. And it's not because they don't like each other; often it's just that they tackle things differently.

Nine-year-olds continue the trend begun by eight-year-olds of gravitating towards their own gender. Nine-year-olds often prefer working with partners, rather than in small groups, and typically they'll want to choose their own partner, usually someone of the same gender. At age nine, this preference for being with the same gender can often take on a mean tone, as children, particularly girls, begin to form cliques.

Teachers of developmental eight- and nine-year-olds will need to be particularly conscious of setting up classroom structures that bring boys and girls together, often in the face of resistance. Building positive relationships between boys and girls at these ages requires constant vigilance. The teacher will need to draw on a wide range of strategies and continually work on helping children form and maintain caring relationships.

Teachers of developmental ten-year-olds will have a somewhat easier time. Tens are more easygoing about everything, including friendships. Generally, boys and girls play well together at this age and enjoy whole-group and small-group activities. However, ten-year-olds are also approaching adolescence, when boy-girl relationships become loaded with cultural and peer expectations about sexuality. Teachers will need to stay alert to heightened sexual tension in relationships between boys and girls at this age.

Children ages eleven and older

At age eleven, boys and girls begin to separate again, partly because of a marked difference in physical development. By eleven, many girls have begun to menstruate; yet puberty is still a few years away for most eleven-year-old boys. Some boys and girls at this age will actively seek ways to be together. But for the rest, it can be a confusing time.

As Chip Wood says, "Watch how children this age come to the meeting circle or to a game: the boys on one side, the girls on another. Boys are watching the girls change and wondering when something is going to happen to them." (Wood 1997, 119) At this age, teachers will need to deliberately create mixed-gender work groups and partnerships in order to bring boys and girls together in positive ways.

The emerging interest in the other gender can also lead to complicated emotions for children this age. The earlier and earlier onset of physical development means that children's bodies have often begun marching resolutely toward adulthood while their minds are still those of children.

By fifth-sixth grade, a number of students may already be facing choices about sexuality—well before they're ready cognitively or emotionally for sexual and romantic relationships. And pop culture's blast of constant messages about sexuality can make life even more confusing. Teachers will need to be aware of this and develop strategies for dealing with some of the difficult situations that boys and girls can face as they begin to navigate new terrain.

Respect family and cultural values

Students in American classrooms come from widely diverse families and communities, with varying ideas and traditions about gender roles and relationships. As teachers try to implement a vision of girls and boys relating to each other as friends and equals rather than as enemies on either side of the "cootie" line, they might face a bewildering array of conflicting family beliefs. The goal is to work towards improving the gender climate in the classroom while at the same time respecting the cultural and family values represented by the students.

The first step is to get to know the families of your students. One way to learn about families is during conference time, preferably early in the year. Invite family members to share their goals for their child. Share your own goals for the year, perhaps including the goal of improving relationships between boys and girls in the classroom. Then listen closely and non-judgmentally to family members' responses, concerns, and questions.

Some teachers send home a letter at the beginning of the year to welcome parents, grandparents, and other caregivers into the classroom. The letter asks if the adults would be willing to volunteer time in the classroom and then asks them to list special talents, skills, interests, or cultural traditions that they would be willing to share. This gives teachers a way to learn about the families. And when family members visit the classroom, they experience firsthand the positive social climate the teacher is trying to create.

Here are some additional ways to learn about students and their families:

- Encourage children to share about cultural traditions and beliefs. This can happen regularly during a daily morning meeting or circle time.

- Early in the year, structure "getting to know you" activities for the children. Here are some examples:

  - On the first day of school, children decorate nametags in a way that tells something about them. For example, a child who loves baseball might draw a picture of a baseball bat next to her name.

  - Children write autobiographies and read them aloud to the group. Teachers can give children a list of guiding questions to help them get started with the writing.

  - Early in the school year, children interview each other, using a designated number of questions (perhaps two for primary grades, three or four for older grades). Questions might include: What's one thing you like to do? What do you like best about where you live? What's your favorite subject in school? Students then introduce one another to the entire class, sharing each other's responses. For example, "This is Alex. He loves to play the trumpet and his favorite subject is art."

◆ Do an activity such as "A Warm Wind Blows" (see description at end of section) in which children learn about shared interests.

• Invite families and community members into the classroom to talk about family and cultural traditions. In addition, to learn more about diversity issues you can visit community cultural centers, attend community events, and take advantage of any multicultural training offered in your district.

Finally, throughout the year, it's important to keep families informed about classroom goals and activities, particularly if you're trying something new. If a parent expresses concern about something that's happening in the classroom, such as Jeremy's father in the opening scenario about the drama corner, try to find a time to talk face-to-face. After listening to parents and making sure that you understand their concerns, respectfully explain your thinking and your goals. Don't hesitate to speak with the voice of authority—the decisions you make about managing your classroom are based on your best knowledge of education and of child development. And then work towards a solution that accommodates everyone's concern for the child.

In addition to meeting with family members in conferences, you can also send families a regular newsletter about classroom life. And you can invite family members to visit the classroom, perhaps during a morning meeting or some other structured activity where they can see how children interact with one another. When you demonstrate respect for families and engage them in the daily life of the classroom, you increase the possibility that they will support your efforts.

Activity

A Warm Wind Blows

Move chairs into a circle. The number of chairs should be one less than the number of participants. Participants sit in the chairs and one person stands in the middle of the circle. The person in the middle says "A warm wind blows for anyone who _____," filling in the blank with a category such as "has a dog." Everyone who fits that category comes into the center of the circle and then quickly finds a new place to sit. The one person who doesn't find a seat now stands in the center of the circle and says "A warm wind blows for anyone who _____," naming a new category. The activity continues for several rounds.

Encourage students to name categories that relate to interests, hobbies, and family rather than clothing or appearance. You could brainstorm a list of categories before beginning the activity.

Work Cited

Wood, Chip. 1997. *Yardsticks: Children in the Classroom Ages 4–14, A Resource for Parents and Teachers*. Greenfield, MA: Northeast Foundation for Children.

Strategy Two: Know Yourself

Between preparing students *for state-wide tests, teaching a new math curriculum, trying different ways to improve literacy, and managing the range of behavior and learning problems that exist in a class where one quarter of the students have individualized learning plans, Mr. Troy sometimes feels like he needs five brains and ten hands. When he attended an in-service presentation on classroom gender relationships, he was intrigued but also skeptical. He wanted to do something about the squabbling, teasing, and taunting that seemed so prevalent among his third grade students. But what could he change? And how would he find the time to work on gender relations when there were so many other demands?*

In the middle of a busy teaching life, it can sometimes feel difficult to step back and assess the needs of the group. And it can be even more challenging to find time for self-assessment. However, self-assessment is important because even the most caring, thoughtful teachers can unintentionally perpetuate gender divisions in the classroom.

Children are always watching you and picking up clues about how to think about themselves and behave towards others. Simple classroom management decisions, such as how you organize children for lining- up, and more subtle choices, such as whom you call on most frequently, can bring boys and girls together—or reinforce their tendency to divide by gender. For this reason, assessing your own beliefs and practices is a critical step to improving gender relationships in the classroom.

Take time for reflection

This assessment doesn't need to be time consuming. In fact, you could pause for just a few minutes right now and do the following:

Imagine you're watching a video of a typical day in your classroom and school, beginning in the morning. Observe yourself and the students through different time periods. As you notice the interactions among the children, ask yourself:

- *How often are boys and girls working and playing separately?*

- *How often are boys and girls working and playing together?*

- *How do girls and boys talk to one another? What words do they use? What tone of voice?*

- *How do boys and girls typically interact with each other? Through friendly, respectful exchanges? Teasing and taunting? Flirting and manipulating?*

- *What is happening between boys and girls outside the classroom, specifically at lunch and recess?*

In just a few minutes, you've had a chance to heighten your awareness of gender relationships in the classroom and at school. Now, take this awareness back into the classroom and observe students—and your interactions with them—in a variety of settings.

During this period of observation, begin to pay attention to the small choices you make that bring boys and girls together in positive, friendly ways—or push them apart. You might ask yourself:

- How do I typically address students?

- How do I typically organize students for lining up or for work groups?

- How do I confront the teasing, taunting, and name-calling that often occur?

- In the books I choose, how are girls, boys, and relationships between the two portrayed?

Do a formal assessment to learn more

Sometimes doing a more formal assessment of management decisions and curriculum choices can help teachers know where to focus their attention. For instance, the assessment might help you see that establishing clear, positive classroom rules is a great way to begin working on gender relationships. Or you might see that in the first weeks of school you need to be more deliberate about mixing boys and girls in work groups. Or you could discover that you need to pay attention to curriculum materials or figure out a different way to prepare children for lunch and recess. Taking the time to reflect on the details of your current practices can give you important information about how to proceed.

The following questionnaire is a useful tool for assessing current practices around gender relationships. To help you identify the areas you most want to work on, each question has a number after it, referring to one of the strategies in this book.

How often do I . . .

• Create rules and routines that ensure a sense of physical and emotional safety for all the children? (3)

> *Always   Frequently   Occasionally   Rarely*

• Help boys and girls get to know each other as individuals? (3)

> *Always   Frequently   Occasionally   Rarely*

• Make gender-integrated seating assignments? (4)

> *Always   Frequently   Occasionally   Rarely*

• Create mixed-gender work groups? (4)

> *Always   Frequently   Occasionally   Rarely*

• Ask children to line up according to interests rather than gender? (4)

> *Always   Frequently   Occasionally   Rarely*

• Assign classroom jobs to mixed-gender teams? (4)

> *Always   Frequently   Occasionally   Rarely*

• Make sure that boys and girls have equal access to all activities at choice time? (4)

> *Always   Frequently   Occasionally   Rarely*

• Have one-on-one and group conversations with students about relationships between boys and girls at school, especially when issues such as teasing and excluding arise? (5)

> *Always   Frequently   Occasionally   Rarely*

- Read or assign books to the class that portray boys and girls in a wide range of roles, including girls as heroes and boys as nurturers? (6)

  Always   Frequently   Occasionally   Rarely

- Read or assign books in which there are strong mixed-gender friendships? (6)

  Always   Frequently   Occasionally   Rarely

- Supplement curriculum materials so that the achievements and struggles of both women and men are honored? (7)

  Always   Frequently   Occasionally   Rarely

- Display images of men and women or boys and girls in nontraditional gender roles and relationships? (8)

  Always   Frequently   Occasionally   Rarely

- Teach, model, and practice safe, respectful lunch and recess behavior? (9, 10)

  Always   Frequently   Occasionally   Rarely

- Provide structures and activities that bring boys and girls together in positive ways during lunch and recess? (9, 10)

  Always   Frequently   Occasionally   Rarely

Responses of "Always" and "Frequently" indicate areas where you're already taking steps to promote positive gender relationships in school. It's important to note these, affirming what's going well. Responses of "Occasionally" and "Rarely" let you know where you might want to focus attention. The strategies that follow will help you think about further steps to take towards bringing boys and girls together.

Classroom Management

Strategy Three:
Provide a Safe Classroom Climate

Strategy Four:
Give Boys and Girls Opportunities to Work and Play Together

Strategy Five:
Facilitate Inclusive Conversations

THE CUMULATIVE EFFECT of a teacher's small daily decisions can be quite powerful. Every decision a teacher makes about classroom routines, structures for grouping students, expectations for behavior, and guidelines for conversations, has a potential impact on how boys and girls interact with one another.

Even something as simple as the first words that a teacher speaks on the first day of school can have a positive or negative effect. "Good morning, boys and girls!" This phrase seems gentle and familiar. But it can send a divisive message:

• The group is divided already on the first day of school.

• Your gender, or the other gender, is being greeted first.

• Gender matters.

A simple change in wording, however, has a positive impact. "Good morning, class!" "Good morning, everyone!" "Good morning, children!" Messages sent by these greetings might include:

• We're all together in one group.

• No one group is more important than another.

• Gender is not a category that matters in this classroom.

So, too, with other decisions about managing life in the classroom: seemingly small changes can have a big impact.

The strategies in this section are intended to help teachers make those small changes. Because children need to feel safe before they can enjoy working and learning together, strategy three talks about establishing classroom rules and providing daily routines that help boys and girls know each other as individuals. Strategy four addresses the myriad decisions that teachers make about how to organize students, all of which can affect gender relationships. And strategy five pays attention to the importance of facilitating good discussions, particularly discussions that make use of teachable moments.

Strategy Three: Provide a Safe Classroom Climate

I
T'S THE FIRST WEEK OF SCHOOL *and the fourth graders in Ms. Tomasso's room have just finished a tour of the room. "As you can see there are lots of exciting things we'll be learning about," Ms. Tomasso says. "One of my hopes this year is that boys and girls will learn and play together in a friendly manner. What's one thing that each of you hopes to accomplish this year in school?" As children respond, Ms. Tomasso writes their answers on a flip chart. Over the next few days, Ms. Tomasso and the children will continue their discussion about hopes for the year, moving from articulating their goals to jointly creating a set of rules that will help them achieve those goals.*

Kara has signed up to share during the class morning meeting. She is a soccer player, known by classmates as a star athlete whose life is centered on practices and games. She wears soccer shorts to school fall, winter, and spring. "I started playing soccer on a traveling team," she begins. "In two weeks we have a game in Agawam. I'm ready for questions and comments. Luke?"

"I play on the rec league team," Luke comments. "How is it different from that?"

"We have to practice twice a week instead of once, and all the away games are out of town," Kara responds. "Megan?"

"Do you have to be really good?" Megan asks.

"Yeah, I had to try out to get on the team. Dante?"

"How do you like it?"

"I like the games, because they're a lot harder than before. But I have to do all my homework in the car. We eat so many hamburgers I never want to see another hamburger, and it takes up my whole Saturday."

Fostering positive relationships between boys and girls happens most easily within a safe framework. In both of the

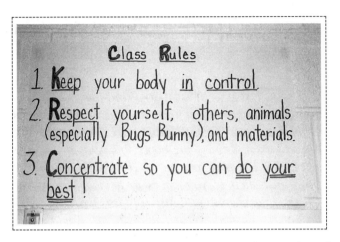

Class Rules
1. Keep your body in control.
2. Respect yourself, others, animals (especially Bugs Bunny), and materials.
3. Concentrate so you can do your best!

classrooms described on the previous page, the teachers have created environments where children feel safe and known. In the first example, the teacher takes time during the early weeks of school to establish rules based on teacher and student goals for the year. In the second example, the teacher provides a daily sharing routine that helps boys and girls know each other as individuals.

Create rules that provide a foundation for respectful interactions

When teachers and students work together to create rules that grow from everyone's goals, students feel more invested in following those rules. Classroom rules are most effective when they are stated positively (focusing on what students *should* do rather than what they *shouldn't* do) and when they are broad enough to encompass a variety of classroom situations. (Brady et al. 2003)

For example, the rules in Maureen Russell's first grade classroom at Kensington Elementary School in Springfield, Massachusetts, are short and sweet: take care of yourself; take care of materials; take care of each other. The process for creating this short list began in the first weeks of school with students brainstorming all the possible rules they felt would be important in helping them achieve their goals for the year. The teacher then helped them consolidate their long list of specific rules into a short list of broadly stated rules.

In older grades, the language used to state the rules might be more sophisticated, but the rules should still address the general areas of respect for self, others, and materials.

Here are some examples of classroom rules that were created collaboratively by teacher and students at various grade levels:

First grade

Make friends with other people.

Take care of our classroom things.

Be good to each other.

Take care of yourself.

Third grade

Take care of everyone.

Take care of everything in our school.

Do your best work.

Fifth grade

We take care of each other and our room.

We treat others how we want to be treated.

We do our best.

Although these classroom rules do not explicitly address boy-girl relationships, they establish the overall expectation that everyone will treat each other kindly and respectfully, regardless of gender or any other potential dividers. "If you set up clear rules and expectations with children, and they're invested in these rules and expectations, you have the groundwork to start from," Russell says. "When important issues and problems come up, you can begin by referring back to your rules: 'Let's look at our rules about this.' or 'Our rules say that. . . .'"

Discuss, model, and practice

In order for rules to be effective, it's important to discuss them, model them, and give students opportunities to practice living them in a wide range of situations. (Brady 2003) For example, students in Russell's class might discuss what exactly "taking care" means in different contexts:

- "What does it mean to take care of each other during our morning meeting time? If we only greet our best friends, are we taking care of each other?"

- "What about during recess? If we only let boys play on our team, are we treating each other with respect?"

- "If Chandra spills her milk in the cafeteria and some kids tease her about it, are they taking care of her?"

Once specific behaviors are named, the teacher models the desired behaviors and then gives children opportunities to practice them. The teacher continually offers guidance in helping students compare their behavior to the "caring" standards set by their rules. Throughout the year, the teacher helps students learn from their mistakes and also affirms their successes. Each "caring decision" along the way serves to reinforce the students' collective notion of themselves as caretakers.

Consistently enforce the rules

Teachers also need to consistently enforce the rules. Students are eagle-eyed witnesses of teacher behavior. Every time a teacher speaks to a boy for teasing a girl about her bra, or sits down with a girl to discuss the "weirdo" note she put in every boy's cubby, students make a mental note: This teacher is paying attention to how we behave. We'd better pay attention, too.

Teasing demands special attention

Establishing, practicing, and reinforcing classroom rules that say, "In this classroom we treat each other with care and respect," will go a long way towards minimizing the teasing that is so prevalent in elementary schools. But teasing demands special attention because it can seriously undermine attempts to bring boys and girls together. Barrie Thorne says:

> Teasing makes cross-gender interaction risky, increases social distance between girls and boys, and has the effect of marking and policing gender boundaries. The risk of being teased may dissuade kids from publicly choosing to be with someone of the opposite gender. (Thorne 1993, 54)

Fifth grade teacher Eric Henry notes that much of the humor in our culture is based on mockery, making it difficult for children to know the difference between gentle and hurtful teasing.

I'm not against playful teasing among friends. I do believe there are places for this kind of gentle and affectionate teasing. However, I don't think my classroom is one of them. The likelihood that playful teasing will go awry is simply too great. There are very subtle distinctions that separate playful bantering from hurtful teasing, distinctions that many adults with strong communication skills. . .have trouble seeing, not to mention fifth-grade students. For this reason, I insist that teasing, playful or not, does not belong in the classroom. (Henry 1999, 4)

From the beginning of the year, Henry lets students know that teasing is not allowed. He clearly defines what he means by teasing—words or actions that lead class members to doubt their worthiness as people or as learners—and he responds consistently when students tease each other. Sometimes a simple reminder, "That's teasing," is enough. Sometimes, he uses logical consequences. He also has regular discussions with the students about the ways in which teasing can be a problem and about calm ways to respond to it. (Henry 1999)

For more information on ways to respond to teasing, please see the Resources section at the end of the book.

Establish rules for specific situations

One morning the meeting circle in Mr. Andrews's third grade classroom formed with girls on one side and boys on the other. "What do you notice about our circle?" he asked. Students fairly quickly sized up the problem. Mr. Andrews reminded the students, "One of our goals this year is for boys and girls to get along well and learn from each other. What do you think we need to do in morning meeting to make sure that happens?" After some deliberation, students made a rule saying that boys and girls needed to sit near enough to talk to each other during morning meeting. "What would that look like, specifically?" Mr. Andrews asked. The students decided that no more than two people of the same gender should sit next to each other. They then quickly adjusted their seating.

In some cases, a class might form habits that are counter-productive to building positive relationships between boys and girls. In these cases, a teacher will want to establish specific rules for specific settings or situations, such as daily meetings or class discussions.

Sometimes teachers will simply set these rules. But teachers can also use a collaborative process to establish these situation-specific rules. As with establishing classroom rules, begin by defining the goals and then ask students to help figure out what rules will help achieve those goals. For example, goals for class discussions might include: to learn from one another; to hear what everyone thinks; to find solutions to problems; to get to know each other better. Some rules to support these goals might include:

• Raise your hand to speak.

• Let each person finish speaking before raising your hand.

• Whether you agree or disagree, do so respectfully.

• Listen quietly when someone is talking.

This rule setting process can also be used to establish specific guidelines for situations outside the classroom, such as lunch or recess.

Establish routines for greeting and sharing

Many elementary school teachers begin the day with circle time or some kind of morning gathering. In the *Responsive Classroom®* approach to teaching, used by many of the teachers interviewed for this book, the daily gathering is called Morning Meeting.

During Morning Meeting, children and teacher gather in a circle for fifteen to thirty minutes at the beginning of each school day to greet each other, share about events in their lives, engage in a group activity, and read a news and announcements chart together. This daily ritual builds a strong sense of community and helps students feel safe and known in school. (Kriete 2002)

The greeting and sharing segments of Morning Meeting, in particular, lend themselves well to helping children bridge the gender gap. But even if you don't hold a morning gathering, you can build in time during the day for a daily greeting routine and a brief personal sharing time.

Greeting

A daily greeting ritual ensures that every child is greeted by name at the beginning of the day. This ritual can help students reach across gender, clique, and friendship lines to extend the range of classmates they notice and greet.

It's easy to build a greeting ritual into an already established circle time or morning gathering. If you don't have a morning gathering, you can still establish a first-thing-in-the-morning greeting routine. Gather students in a circle and teach a simple greeting for starters. A "Hello, Joe" or "Good morning, Marcia" accompanied by a gentle handshake is a good one to begin with. Talk with students about the importance of greeting each other in a friendly and respectful way. Some specific guidelines can include:

- Use the person's name. (If you forget it, softly ask the person to tell you.)
- Look at the person when you're greeting them.
- Use a gentle handshake.

It's also important to establish the role of the rest of the group when someone is being greeted. That is, students who are not being greeted or doing the greeting should sit quietly, watch the greeting go around the circle, and most importantly, not laugh if someone makes a mistake. This is critical, as children will often make mistakes while greeting one another, especially at the beginning when everyone is feeling a bit awkward. Students must know that they can forget a name or say the wrong name or get their words or handshake mixed up without anyone making fun of them.

Another thing to pay attention to is that boys don't always greet other boys and girls other girls. Sometimes this means

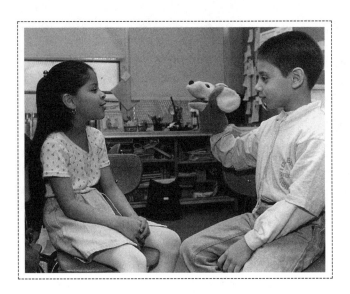

requiring students to sit boy–girl in the meeting circle. You can also specify that students pass a greeting in a mixed-gender pattern rather than simply going around the circle.

Once the group becomes comfortable with greeting one another, the greetings can become more elaborate and playful, incorporating creative handshakes or taking the form of a chant or song. At the end of this chapter, you'll find a list of ten greetings, some simple, some elaborate. For a more extensive list of greetings, take a look at *The Morning Meeting Book* by Roxann Kriete or *The First Six Weeks of School* by Paula Denton and Roxann Kriete. You can also make up your own greetings with the students.

Sharing

A daily sharing ritual gives students an opportunity to learn about each other's lives and experiences, to recognize commonalities and differences, and view one another as complex individuals. In the opening scenario about Kara, the soccer player, the class learned that Kara had achieved something difficult. They also learned that along with this achievement came ongoing effort. Their image of Kara is now complicated and enriched—she's a star athlete who constantly juggles the demands of her sport with the demands of school. By getting to know Kara better, the students can see her as more than simply a representative of a label such as gender.

During sharing, a student briefly presents a piece of news, and then asks for a few questions and comments. Students are taught to ask respectful questions that open up the topic or to make empathic comments. The skills of clearly presenting information, asking relevant questions, and offering meaningful comments are complex ones that children develop over time through the daily practice of the sharing ritual.

Springfield, Massachusetts, teacher Tina Valentine is a vocal advocate of sharing:

Sharing helps kids understand and learn about each other. The students talk about what's happening in their lives, or they bring in an item that's related to their topic for sharing, such as a hobby or sports accomplishment. They learn how to listen well, ask respectful questions, and make thoughtful and empathic comments. It's a great way to help children learn to be respectful of each other.

As with a greeting ritual, you can build sharing into an established daily gathering. But even if you don't have an established meeting time, you can provide a short period of time each day (perhaps after lunch) for a few children to share personal news. Students can sign up ahead of time so they come prepared and the sharing doesn't go on for too long on any one day.

It is important to distinguish between this kind of sharing and the traditional "show and tell." In sharing, the focus is on the child's experiences and thoughts; in show and tell the focus is on a child's possession. In many classrooms that use this approach to sharing, teachers and students brainstorm a list of possible subjects. Many teachers prohibit toys of any sort and ask families for help enforcing this. It often helps to send a letter home to families explaining the purposes of sharing and offering a list of possible topics.

It does take time to teach children how to share appropriately. Selecting news to share, presenting the news clearly, listening respectfully, asking pertinent questions, and making empathic comments are all sophisticated communication and social skills. In order for sharing to be a positive experience, teachers should model each aspect of sharing and then practice repeatedly with the children, asking questions such as, "How do you know when someone is listening carefully?" and "What does a respectful question sound like?" The payoff is worth the time. Not only do children get to know each other better, they also learn critical thinking, presentation, and discussion skills that will help in all areas of the curriculum.

Activities

"Good Morning" Greeting

This is the most basic greeting, making it a great greeting for the beginning of the year. Two students face each other, make eye contact, smile, and say, "Good morning, _____," using each other's first name.

Some variations to use early in the year:

• With a wave

• With a salute

• With a bow

• With a thumbs up

• With a peace sign

After a few weeks, when students are more comfortable with each other and with the basic greeting components, you might add the following variations:

• With a handshake

• With a handshake that students make up

• With a high five

• With a high five and ankle shake

• With a pinky shake

• With a touch on the shoulder

• With an elbow shake

Name Card Greeting

Place name cards in the center of the circle. Turn over the top card. The student whose name is on that card begins the greeting. That student turns over the next card in the stack and greets that child. That child then turns over the next card, and so on. When all the cards have been used, the greeting ends with the last child greeting the first child.

Number Greeting

Place numbered slips of paper in a basket. Decide what numbers to use based on the size of your class and the size of the groups that will be greeting each other. For example, if you have twenty-four group members and you want pairs to greet each other, you'll number two sets of slips one through twelve. If you have twenty-four group members and you want groups of four to greet each other, you'll number four sets of slips one through six.

After each group member has drawn a number from the basket, you call out a number. Everyone holding that number comes to the center of the circle to greet each other.

African Greeting

This greeting uses two phrases: *"Sawa bona,"* which means "I see you," and *"Sacona,"* which means "I am here."

All members of the circle close their eyes. The person who begins the greeting opens his/her eyes, turns to the person to the right or left, says *"Sawa bona,* (neighbor's first name)." That student then opens her/his eyes and responds, *"Sacona,* (greeter's first name)."

The greeting then continues around the circle until all members have been greeted.

Cross-Circle Greeting

Children greet someone sitting across the circle from them. There can be many variations on this, such as cross-circle boy/girl greeting, cross-circle someone-you-haven't-spoken-to-yet-this-morning greeting, etc.

Alphabetical Greeting

In this greeting, students say "Good morning" to each other in alphabetical order, being sure to use each other's first name. If students are just learning to alphabetize, it's best if you begin by greeting the student whose name comes first in the alphabet (or asking the students who should go first). With students who are more experienced with alphabetizing, you can begin anywhere in the circle. For example, if Lindsey is the first greeter, she greets Mark, who then looks for the person whose name would be next in alphabetical order. But when it gets to Will, he might find that he needs to go back to the beginning of the alphabet and greet Annie. This greeting can take a while to complete.

Snowball Greeting

Each student writes his/her name on a sheet of paper and crumbles it up so that it looks like a snowball. Students then toss the crumbled pieces of paper into the center of the circle. Students pick up a snowball that has landed near them and open the paper. The student who begins the greeting then walks over to the student whose name s/he has and says "Good morning, _____." The first student returns to his/her place in the circle and the student who was greeted finds the student whose name is on her/his snowball and greets that student, and so on until everyone has been greeted.

Variation: After the initial round of greetings, students recrumble the papers that they're holding and toss them. Each student picks up a new snowball, reads the name, and then respectfully watches that student for the rest of the day, with a goal of noticing something positive. At the end of the day, the class circles up and each student pays a compliment to the classmate s/he observed.

Hello, Neighbor

Students stand and form an inner and an outer circle. The inside circle faces the outer circle. Students who are facing each other are now partners who greet each other with the following chant. The inside circle then moves one person to the right so that everyone has a new partner and repeats the chant. This continues until everyone is back in her/his original place.

Hello, neighbor, what d'ya say? (Wave to your partner.)

It's gonna be a wonderful day. (Arms circle over head and then move down to the sides.)

Clap your hands and boogie on down. (Clap hands and wiggle down.)

Give me a bump and turn around. (Gently bump hips.)

Variation 1: Instead of bumping hips, students can jump ("Give me a jump and turn around") or raise hands high ("Then raise your hands and turn around").

Variation 2: *Hey there,* (partner's first name), *what d'ya say?*

It's gonna be a dynamite day.

Grab your hands. (Partners join hands.)

And circle around. (Partners gently swing each other in a circle.)

Reach real high. (Each person raises hands over head.)

And boogie on down. (Wiggle down.)

Cheer Greeting

Going around the circle, students do the following call-and-response greeting:

S[tudent]–*My name is* (first name).

G[roup]–*YEAH!*

S–*And I like to* (activity).

G–*Uh-huh.*

S–*And I'll be a* (person who does this activity).

G–*YEAH!*

S–*Every day of my life.*

G–*Every day of* (his/her) *life.*

For example:

My name is Carla.

YEAH!

And I like to swim.

Uh-huh.

And I'll be a swimmer.

YEAH!

Every day of my life.

Every day of her life.

Skip Greeting

In this greeting, the child who begins announces the number of spaces that will be skipped. For example, the child says "Skip four," and then walks to the fifth person in the circle and greets him/her. The greeter then takes that person's place and the student who was greeted walks to the fifth person down, greets and switches places, and so on until everyone has been greeted. The greeting will flow around the circle several times. Before the greeting begins, work with the class to figure out how many spaces to skip based on the number of people in the circle that day. The challenge is to make sure that everyone gets greeted.

Works Cited

Brady, Kathryn, Mary Beth Forton, Deborah Porter, and Chip Wood. 2003. *Rules in School.* Greenfield, MA: Northeast Foundation for Children.

Henry, Eric. 1999. "But I Was Only Joking! How One Teacher Confronts Teasing in a Fifth Grade Classroom." *Responsive Classroom: A Newsletter for Teachers.* (Spring): 4–5. Northeast Foundation for Children.

Kriete, Roxann. 2002. *The Morning Meeting Book.* Greenfield, MA: Northeast Foundation for Children.

Thorne, Barrie. 1993. *Gender Play: Girls and Boys in School.* New Brunswick, NJ: Rutgers University Press.

Strategy Four: Give Boys and Girls Opportunities to Work and Play Together

M R. OWEN RINGS THE CHIME. *As the tone reverberates and gradually disappears, the chattering fifth graders, who have just returned from lunch, quiet down and turn their attention to the teacher. "Welcome back, everyone! We're going to spend the first part of the afternoon starting a math project. I've placed you in new work groups so listen up."*

A hand shoots into the air. "Mr. Owen," Ian says, "I really like working with Dave. Can't we work together again?"

"You'll get to work with Dave again at some point, don't worry. But it's early in the year and I want you and everyone in the class to have opportunities to work with lots of different students. So, Ian, for this project I'd like you to work with Shandra and Casey; Suky, Craig, and Sara will work together . . . "

Down the hall, the students in Ms. Petroskey's second grade classroom are lining up to go to the music room. "Everyone who has a furry pet get in line," Ms. Petroskey says. Several boys and girls scurry to get in line and quickly start talking with each other about their beloved cats, dogs, and hamsters.

"Now everyone who has a scaly pet get in line." Two children join the line, surprised to find that they have a love of snakes in common.

"Okay, now everyone who has no pet get in line." Several more children join; a boy and a girl begin talking about what kind of pet they'd like to have someday.

"What have I left out?" Ms. Petroskey asks. "Birds," Anita says. "Right. Everyone who has a feathered pet get in line." Anita and three other classmates line up.

Throughout the day, teachers need to organize students for seating, lining up, grouping, and partnering. This provides many opportunities to bring boys and girls together in positive ways so that they learn about, and from, a wide range of classmates. While students may resist this at times, eventually they begin to take for granted that groups and lines will be gender-integrated. Working and playing with students of the other gender simply becomes "part of the air they breathe," an expected part of life at school.

Line students up by interests rather than gender

Lining up can be accomplished efficiently with no reference to gender. "The only boy–girl division I make in my classroom is for the bathroom," first grade teacher Maureen Russell notes, "and then only because the bathrooms are so far apart!" Instead of organizing students by gender, she and many teachers focus on individual identities and interests. This makes gender irrelevant and heightens students' awareness of the things they have in common. For example, here's a list of sorting categories that teachers might use when asking students to line up:

Please line up, everyone who…

- Is wearing (sneakers, boots, sandals)
- Has a first name starting with (A–M, N–Z)
- Likes (macaroni, hamburgers, tuna fish)
- Loves the color (blue, red, purple)
- Loves (roller coasters, Ferris wheels, merry-go-rounds)
- Has (0–1 siblings, 2 or more siblings)
- Is an (oldest, youngest, middle) child
- Has a (winter, spring, summer, fall) birthday
- Has moved to a different town at least once
- Plays a musical instrument, plays basketball, collects rocks, etc.

Tina Valentine has noticed that when fourth graders begin the year lining up in this way, it affects their attitude:

Simple things, like lining up according to birthdays or favorite foods, helps kids realize you can line up next to lots of different children, not just your best friends. Kids stop being reluctant to stand next to someone they don't know well. When you make it fun, kids realize, "Hey, it's kind of cool, finding out about other people's interests." Instead of having all-boy and all-girl groupings, we have interest groupings.

Assign seating with an eye to integrating boys and girls

Most often in elementary school, seats are assigned. Students assume this, so seating provides an excellent opportunity to actively and creatively mix girls and boys. Girl-boy or even girl-girl/boy-boy patterns can be protocol for morning meetings or circle time, providing a consistent place and time where boys and girls can get to know each other informally.

During instructional time, whether students sit in rows or small table clusters, you'll want to take a variety of factors into account when you assign seats. Early in the year, as you're getting to know the students, you might create a seating chart based on the alphabet or birth dates. Although this won't result in an evenly alternating boy-girl pattern, it will avoid students clustering in best friend groupings.

When you get to know students better, you can begin to take common interests and skills into account along with a desire to mix genders. Later in the year, you can also ask the students for creative ideas for "mixing it up." Whatever system you use, change seating assignments and patterns frequently so that everyone gets a chance to work with everyone else.

Assign girl-boy partners for classroom jobs

Think for a few moments about who typically does what job in the classroom. Are there any patterns you notice? Do you find yourself calling just on boys to do physical chores, such as putting chairs on tables or carrying sports equipment, or just girls to hang artwork or take roll? If so, you'll want to pay attention to this and devise a system that allows children to rotate through all the classroom chores.

Also, consider implementing a system that assigns girls and boys as partners for daily chores. Having girls and boys work together on a shared task is a great way to break down gender barriers and encourage positive relationships. Rather than assigning an individual student to each job, create a chart that assigns partners to daily jobs. Partners can be changed periodically so that many different combinations of boys and girls have the opportunity to work together.

Be mindful when forming partners and groups

Susan Pelis, primary grade teacher, uses the word "mindful" to describe the way she groups and partners students throughout the year. "There's a natural flow of boys and girls together for field trips, lunch inviting, reading groups, and choice time over the course of the year," she says. "But it doesn't happen by chance; the teacher needs to direct the process."

Intentional grouping combats the status quo, the homogeneous combinations that usually result when a teacher just says "Buddy up!" or "Get in groups of four!" In the case of games or contests, it also avoids pitting boys and girls *against* each other.

Upper grades teacher Anna Foot says, "In competitive situations, if you let the teams be divided by gender, boys against the girls or vice versa, the stakes are too high: it matters too much who wins. On the other hand, if it's just a group of ten random kids on a team, who wins becomes far less important."

From the beginning of the year, Foot sets the expectation that boys and girls will be doing things together in her classroom:

> We do a partner activity at the beginning of the year where students have to find out about each other. I deliberately match girls with boys. My feeling is that if you expect something from kids, they'll nearly always do it. But you need to clearly let them know what it is that you expect, and then set it up so that they can really do it. You can't say to yourself, "Okay, this year I want all of the boys and girls to talk to each other," and then just expect it to happen.

Foot believes that students actually like it when teachers require them to work with students of the other gender. "It gives them something concrete to do together and something specific to talk about," she says. "It takes away the awkwardness." Also, because it's required, it's safe. No one can tease anyone about sitting with a boy or girl, because everyone is.

Teachers sometimes use a "clock buddies" activity to help students choose a wide variety of partners. Early in the year, the teacher gives students a piece of paper with a clock face drawn on it and a line next to twelve, three, six, and nine. (Later in the year, the teacher might add lines next to the other hours.) Each student makes an "appointment" with four different students and writes that student's name on the appropriate line. The two students must be sure to write down each other's name so that no one "double books."

Teachers can use a variety of criteria to help students choose buddies other than their best friends. (For example, "For your twelve o'clock buddy choose someone who has the same color eyes as you; for your three o'clock buddy choose someone whose last name has the same number of letters as yours; for your six o'clock buddy choose someone of a different gender; etc.") Teachers model and practice how to invite someone to be a clock buddy and how to respond to an invitation. Once the forms are completed, students keep them in their folders for future reference when the teacher says, "Today in math I want you to work with your six o'clock buddy."

Below are a few other ideas for grouping and partnering students:

- Form groups or partners based on your knowledge of students' shared interests. You might even challenge the group to figure out what they have in common.

- Form groups or partners based on knowledge of students' complementary strengths.

- Form groups or partners using an arbitrary system, such as having students pick numbers or count off. If you use an arbitrary system you might want to keep track of the groupings so that the same children don't end up together over and over again.

Teach children how to choose their own work partners

In Mr. Titus's fourth grade classroom, the students are getting ready to show what they have learned about action verbs. The students will choose how to demonstrate what they've learned and they'll choose work partners. "Think carefully about what you're going to do and how you'll choose a partner," Mr. Titus urges. "Who can remind us about what makes a good partner?"

Students think briefly and then hands go up.

"If you're good at spelling and they're good at drawing, you can share."

"Someone who listens to your ideas and you listen to theirs."

"Someone who will work hard and not distract you."

Students then have two minutes to find a partner and begin planning. Hannah chooses Enrico; Jamul and Sarah gravitate towards each other; and wiggly Joey says "yes" when Alison approaches him. Pairs gather materials and get to work.

As the year goes on, you can encourage children to choose their own work partners, making choices based on criteria you've established together. Giving students the opportunity to think about and name the qualities of a good partner can help them move beyond simply choosing their best friend, who in older grades is often a same gender friend. By working with many different partners, children develop important relationship skills. They get to stretch their capacity to take different roles: to be the one who generates ideas or the one who listens; to be the problem-solver, the organizer, the illustrator, or the writer. Children gain an awareness of their own resources and the flexibility to adapt to others' styles and strengths.

Early in the year, third grade teacher Carolyn Bush teaches the students how to choose good work partners. She and the students discuss what to look for in a partner. She asks students to reflect on their own abilities and then think about what a partner could provide. After discussing ideas, they make a list of possible complementary strengths to look for in a partner. For example, if a project involves making a poster and you're a good speller but have a hard time drawing, you might look for a partner who has artistic ability. After Bush and the children have discussed the criteria in depth, the children practice choosing a partner and then write a paragraph about why they chose that particular person for that project. With this sort of ongoing conscious attention to forming solid working partnerships based on interests and skills, students get to know each other in new and different ways. Fifth grade teacher Jane Stephenson says, "When children work together, they hear each other's ideas and learn about each other's talents. Then they might realize, 'Oh, he's a good artist' or 'She likes to write song lyrics.' Friendships often develop from students learning about each other's interests and skills."

In addition to discussing and practicing how to decide on a good partner, teachers can teach, model, and practice how to ask someone to work with you, how to reply to an invitation to work with someone, and how to reflect later on the working relationship.

At choice time give boys and girls opportunities to work on a variety of tasks with a range of partners

Allowing children to follow their natural inclinations for choice time often draws an invisible line down the middle of the classroom, as boys flock to the blocks and girls gather around the paints, or boys to the math games and girls to the writing center. Although it's not always easy or comfortable to mix up the genders at choice time, it's worth persevering in the face of student resistance. Terry Kayne, second-third grade teacher, says, "While I sometimes feel like Sisyphus rolling that ball up a hill, the reality is that friendships between boys and girls begin inside the classroom, at a table doing work."

Below are a few ideas for "mixing things up" during times of the day when children have choices:

- Organize the activities so that—within a framework of choice—each person tries everything. Some teachers set up a chart so that each child knows s/he needs to choose each activity once before doing any activity a second time.

- Teach each activity directly, one at a time, so that all students have the skills needed to choose that activity. Early in the school year, as part of introducing choice time, introduce the activity areas to the whole group and require every student to try each area at least once, so that all students feel comfortable in the area and understand how to use the materials there.

• Give extra encouragement and guidance to children who are doing work that doesn't come naturally to them. For example, with some extra support from the teacher, a child who doesn't usually turn to building projects may come to enjoy them and discover new skills and interests.

In conclusion, here's a reflection from Ruth Sidney Charney, long-time classroom teacher, on a knitting program started years ago by a male teaching intern in her second-third grade classroom:

> Once the children learned the basics, we set up a "Who are our team of experts?" list: who knows how to cast on; who knows how to untangle a knot; etc. There were charts on the board where people could find out who to consult about the end-knot problem or the knit vs. purl question. What was amazing was who ended up on these charts, definitely not the people you would have expected. In fact, most of the "resident experts" were children who would never have signed up for knitting if given a choice. And what pride they showed, when someone came to them and said, "Mickey, could you help me to cast on? I don't know how to get started."
>
> I think that project also broke down some of the stereotypes that many people have that small, detailed handwork requiring fine-motor skills is the purview of girls. A guy was teaching it and everybody was doing it—they could all see themselves as knitters. It made a stunning picture, at quiet time, when everyone in the class got out their knitting. I'll never forget it.

Activity

Three Question Interview

Each child in the circle should have pencil and paper. Have children pair up with a child they don't know very well. The children in the pairs interview each other, asking three simple questions, such as, "What is a movie that you like?" or "What do you like to do after school?" The person asking the questions jots down the person's responses. When both people have had a chance to ask three questions, they find other partners and repeat the process. If you're trying to improve relationships between boys and girls, you could ask children to choose at least one partner of the opposite gender.

After fifteen to twenty minutes, or when each person has had a chance to interview several others, everyone returns to the large circle. Go around the circle. Each child says his/her name, and then you say, "What do people know about _____?" People who interviewed that child share what they learned. Allow time for each person to have a turn.

Variation

This variation works well early in the year, particularly if there are second language learners in the class. Each child interviews a partner and then introduces the partner to the group, using the following fill-in-the-blanks statements.

"This is my friend _____ and her/his favorite activity to do is _____."

You could substitute the following for favorite activity:

• Favorite book

• Favorite food

• Something the child is good at

Strategy Five: Facilitate Inclusive Conversations

M<small>R.</small> D<small>ELGADO</small> *was on playground duty when he heard several girls from his second grade class chanting:*

Girls go to college

to get more knowledge.

Boys go to Jupiter

to get more stupider.

He and the students had been working hard to improve gender relationships in their classroom and he was dismayed to hear this mean-spirited rhyme. He went up to the girls and said, "I know you're having a good time. But you're making fun of the boys. Remember what we've been talking about in class? Is there another chant that wouldn't make fun of anyone?"

"We're just joking around, Mr. Delgado," Sonia said.

"I know. But it's hurtful joking. What's another chant that would be fun?" The girls shrugged and went over to join a game of foursquare.

Later, in the classroom, Mr. Delgado said, "I've noticed a rhyme being chanted on the playground that puts boys down. I know that it seems like just joking around but I think the chant could make people feel bad, too. What do other people think about this?" Framing the question in this way included students as participants in a process of inquiry, which then opened the door to collaborating on a solution. In the end, students in this classroom decided to make up their own playground chants that didn't make fun of anyone and mirrored the syllable pattern in the chant above.

When something happens during the school day to focus attention on cross-gender perceptions and relationships, you have a teachable moment; you can address the behavior in the moment and use it as an opportunity to open up a whole-class discussion.

Teachable moments often spring from small events. You might notice students' discomfort with something that happens in a book the class is reading, or see a group of friends exclude someone from their work group, or overhear a hurtful chant on the playground, as in the example above. Physical education teacher Mark Farnsworth sees conversations that spring from teachable moments as being at the heart of building positive relationships between boys and girls:

> When a teachable moment arises, I think it's important to be ready to facilitate a meaningful conversation about the issue. That way you handle things from a base of community, not autocratic authority.

Practice the art of discussion

Good conversation is an important tool for bridging the gender gap, whether you're talking about where students sit at meeting or a book's stereotypical portrayal of boys or girls. And as any person skilled in any area knows, success with easier tasks comes before success with harder ones. Before children can have meaningful discussions about difficult issues, they need to grow comfortable with everyday conversations with the teacher and with each other. They also need to develop their listening and speaking skills.

Early in the year the teacher should model, and the class should practice, good listening and speaking habits. Questions to ask the students might include:

- *When someone is speaking, how can we show that we are listening?*

It's helpful for students, especially in the primary grades, to articulate and practice the specific behaviors, such as looking at the person who is talking, turning your body toward the person, and keeping your body still.

- *What can we do if we disagree with someone or have something to add?*

Again, ask students to list specific guidelines, such as, "Wait until the person is done talking," "Raise your hand calmly," and "Start with a respectful phrase." You can ask students to give examples of words to use when they disagree: "I have a different idea" or "I want to add something," are more respectful than "That's wrong," or "You forgot to say..."

- *When it's your turn to speak, what kind of voice do you think you should use?*

Ideas might include, "Speak loudly enough for everyone to hear," "Use a regular talking voice," and "Use a friendly and respectful voice."

Students can practice these skills during low stakes discussions in which everyone participates. Teachers who use the *Responsive Classroom®* Morning Meeting structure find that the sharing component offers a great place to practice the skills of respectful discussion.

Gradually, as students become better able to conduct a conversation, and as they grow to know each other better and begin to take for granted that *in this class, we talk about important stuff,* more and more interesting and complicated issues can be brought to the table for group input.

Establish and enforce ground rules for discussion

No matter how well the students have practiced the skills of conversation, discussions about difficult topics can fall apart without ground rules to set the tone. Students will be most likely to remember and follow the ground rules if they've had a hand in establishing them. So, as with classroom rules, clarify the goals of class discussions and then work together to create positive rules that support those goals.

If the goal is to have calm and democratic discussions in which everyone's voice can be heard, the ground rules might include:

- Let each person finish speaking.

- Whether you agree or disagree, do so respectfully.

- If someone makes a mistake, be quiet so the person can rethink the answer.

- Listen quietly when someone is talking.

- Raise your hand to speak.

- Only one person speaks at a time.

- Give everyone a chance to speak.

Any ground rules you establish for conversation should be based on respect for and encouragement of classmates. Once the rules are in place, really act on them. Ruth Sidney Charney urges teachers to help children be responsible for abiding by their conversational rules. "If you give an answer and it's wrong and everybody can laugh at it, or if you share a painting you've done and someone makes a wisecrack and gets away with it, that's a message the teacher is sending." Charney cautions teachers to closely monitor the tone of group conversations to best encourage, rather than discourage, children's participation. She notes:

> We are trying to teach respect and empathy, and taking care of each other and ourselves. When the sarcastic, quick joke, put-down mode takes over, then students aren't taken care of. They're shut down, because the fear of being ridiculed, of making a mistake is very powerful, particularly for girls.

Pay attention to who talks—and how often

Even with clearly established ground rules, there might be a vocal minority that dominates discussions. And despite a teacher's best intentions, it is almost impossible to ignore waving hands, impatient flounces and sighs, and cries of "Me! Me! Me!" from the more eager or assertive students. Teachers can eliminate, or at least decrease, the "call on me" competition by relying on the class roster or simply calling on students at random. Or teachers can give students some alternatives to vigorous hand waving. For example, students who want to speak can:

- Use a thumbs-up signal

- Cross their arms on their chests

- Raise a hand only partway up, without any waving or accompanying sounds

Another possibility is to teach students nonverbal ways to contribute to the conversation. For example, in many classrooms, students use hand signals to show that they strongly agree with something the speaker has said (thumbs-up), strongly disagree (thumbs-down), or have had a similar experience (rock the hand back and forth).

Some teachers pass out slips of paper, cards, or Popsicle sticks, three to a student. Students "spend" their tokens by saying something in a discussion. Students who use up all their tokens need to wait until other students have spoken before joining the discussion again. This both encourages reluctant speakers and reminds willing speakers to edit and prioritize their contributions.

Mark Farnsworth sometimes uses "little one-word shares," in which everyone in the circle uses one word to describe an experience (for example, how it felt to participate in an activity that involved a lot of teamwork). Other times, he uses an object, such as a ball covered with smiley faces, which students pass around the circle or roll to each other. The student who receives the share ball has an opportunity to speak. "Mr. Smiley prompts a lot of participation because students want to hold onto it," Farnsworth says. "It's a really desirable object. It helps control calling out, and there's much more involvement in discussions." With older students, you could pass an unmarked ball or a talking stick.

Teach students how to use "I-statements"

As students become more skilled at discussion and begin to tackle more difficult topics, they might need some specific words and phrases they can use, particularly when angry, hurt feelings surface. Paula Denton, co-author of *The First Six Weeks of School,* teaches students to use I-statements. Although she uses this primarily as a conflict resolution strategy for problems between two students, it can be adapted for use in a group discussion.

She begins by giving students a formula: "When you _____, I feel _____ because _____. So, what I would like is _____." Students practice with positive and low threat I-statements: "When you giggle, I feel happy, because it makes me giggle, too. So, what I would like is for you to keep on giggling." The student who is receiving the I-statement repeats it to make sure s/he heard it accurately. Gradually, students can express more serious feelings. For example, a girl who has been told she can't play soccer with some boys might say to one of the boys, "When you wouldn't let me play soccer, I felt sad and mad because I like to play. So, what I would like is for you and your friends to let me play."

Students brainstorm adjectives to describe feelings: angry, pleased, frustrated, satisfied, annoyed, delighted, embarrassed, proud, unhappy, happy, etc. They also focus on listening carefully and non-defensively. (Denton and Kriete 2000) Primary grade teacher Susan Pelis feels that I-statements can even be used at the K–1 level, to encourage children to use feeling words instead of taunts or punches to communicate during times of conflict.

Conduct problem-solving class meetings

Some teachers use a structured class meeting format to talk about and resolve issues that affect the entire class. Class meetings can be a regularly scheduled event or an occasional, as-needed gathering. They can be preventive, in anticipation of a change in routine or a possibly problematic situation, or they can be reactive, responding to a conflict or ongoing problem.

The Resources section at the end of the book lists several excellent books that describe in detail how to hold class meetings. The following guidelines give the essential elements common to all these approaches:

Establish ground rules for class meetings.

This ensures that the meetings are emotionally and physically safe, and that they run smoothly and effectively. Ground rules should emphasize care and problem-solving rather than blame and punishment.

Establish procedures for class meetings.

For example: participants sit in a circle; the teacher facilitates; there's a reasonable time limit; everyone has an opportunity to contribute ideas or information.

Be sure the problem is developmentally appropriate and affects all or most students.

Class meeting is not the time to talk about a problem between two or three students.

Think about the timing of the meeting.

Do students need to "cool down" before they can discuss the problem?

Only bring issues to class meeting for which you really want student input.

If you've already decided on a solution, then the topic is not appropriate for class meeting.

At the beginning of the meeting, objectively describe the problem and review ground rules.

For example, if Mr. Delgado, the teacher in the opening scenario, regularly heard reports about mean-spirited rhymes on the playground, he might call a class meeting. "Over the past few days, several students have come to talk to me about rhymes and chants that they hear on the playground. These chants sometimes say mean things about boys or girls. The students who have come to talk with me aren't sure how to

respond or what to do when they hear these things. But before we begin talking, who can remind me about the ground rules for class meeting?"

**Encourage non-judgmental sharing
of concerns and feelings about the issue.**

This is a great time to remind students about using "I-messages" to talk about feelings.

**Brainstorm possible solutions and
work towards consensus on a solution to try.**

Solutions need to be workable and realistic, respectful of all, and in accordance with school rules.

Decide how you're going to evaluate the solution.

How will you know it is working? When do you need to evaluate it?

Give older children the language to describe their experience of friendship

Sometimes the biggest problem is not knowing how to talk about what is going on in boy-girl relationships. Most teachers of older elementary age children have probably had the experience of feeling as though the students sometimes are speaking in code. "Joey likes you," one eleven-year-old girl teases another. This seems like a fairly straightforward statement that doesn't warrant the resulting angry blush and extreme statement, "Well, I hate him." At this age, children are beginning to view the opposite gender as intriguing but they're often not sure what sort of relationships to have: Can they just be friends? What do they do about the early stirrings of sexuality? How do they talk about their relationships with each other?

Raphaela Best, a reading specialist and author of *We've All Got Scars,* feels that conversation about gender relationships is important—and increasingly difficult as children move towards early adolescence. She wondered if giving children the language to describe what they were experiencing might help them better understand their relationships with each other.

She began by helping students examine the words they used. "What do you mean when you talk about boys liking girls and girls liking boys?" The students drew a blank. Finally, one boy blurted out, "In our class, it means loving a girl." The terms "hate" and "don't like" were similarly confusing.

Over time, Best persisted in this line of questioning:

- When you are teased for liking someone and you protest that you don't, do you really mean that you don't like them at all or merely that you don't want people to think that you're boyfriend and girlfriend?
- Why do you say that you hate someone you really like?
- Shouldn't you be able to like someone without people bothering you about it?

Best conducted these conversations with the same group of students over the span of three years, from fourth through sixth grade. Although progress was sometimes slow, by sixth grade real friendships between the genders were common, and underground friendships were acknowledged publicly. And, in this year of awakening hormones and "going steady," students were able to bring their own experience to bear in distinguishing between friendship and "something more." (Best 1989)

Best was fortunate in being able to work with the students for three years in a row. Yet experiences such as hers happen every year in classrooms across the country, where teachers get into the habit of talking with children and teaching them how to talk with each other.

Works Cited

Best, Raphaela. 1989. *We've All Got Scars: What Boys and Girls Learn in Elementary School*. Bloomington, IN: Indiana University Press.

Denton, Paula and Roxann Kriete. 2000. *The First Six Weeks of School*. Greenfield, MA: Northeast Foundation for Children.

The Curriculum

Strategy Six:
Provide Balance in the Reading Library

Strategy Seven:
Find Ways to Supplement Textbooks

Strategy Eight:
Pay Attention to What's on the Walls and Shelves

IN ORDER FOR girls and boys to form positive relationships with each other, they need to see each other—and themselves—as complete and valued individuals. In her essay "Curriculum as Window and Mirror," Emily Style draws the analogy of the formal curriculum being a structure that students live in during the school year, inside of which are both windows and mirrors. The windows allow children to see into others' lives; the mirrors allow them to see themselves. Style writes: "White males find, in the house of curriculum, many mirrors to look in, and few windows which frame others' lives." While women, as well as men of color, she continues, "...find almost no mirrors of themselves in the house of curriculum; for them it is often all windows."

This unbalanced curriculum limits both boys and girls. When girls primarily look through windows at male accomplishments, they "are taught their 'proper role' as spectators...," notes Style. And when boys primarily see their own experience reflected back to them, rather than being exposed to the experiences of a wide variety of men and women, they "are narrowly and provincially educated to see themselves as the only real players on life's stage." (Style 1996)

As teachers, our challenge is to provide students with a balanced curriculum, one that offers all children both mirrors *and* windows. This will help girls and boys gain a deeper understanding of and respect for each other, as well as a broader vision of themselves. As you think about how to build bridges across the gender gap, take some time to consider the materials and content of the formal curriculum. Although there may be little flexibility in your state or district mandated curriculum, the following strategies offer suggestions for making changes within the structure of existing curricula.

Work Cited

Style, Emily. 1996. "Curriculum as Window and Mirror." Retrieved July 3, 2002, from National S.E.E.D. Project on Inclusive Curriculum, Wellesley Centers for Women website: www.wcwonline.org/seed/curriculum.html. (Originally published in a monograph, *Listening for All Voices*. 1988. Summit, NJ: Oak Knoll School.)

Strategy Six: Provide Balance in the Reading Library

RECENTLY, a mother and her six-year-old daughter came home from the bookstore, very excited to have found a book of stories called *Girls to the Rescue* (see reading list, page 69), a collection of retold fairy tales and original stories with female protagonists. As they went in the house, prepared to settle on the couch for a good read, the daughter said, "Mama, that's kind of a funny title! It always seems like it's boys who rescue people."

Any teacher familiar with the literature used in most elementary schools won't be surprised by this observation. Even J.K. Rowling's *Harry Potter* series portray a man's world: both the hero and the villain are male, the headmaster is male, Harry's helpers and inspirations are mostly male, his various enemies are male. On the plus side, Harry has a good female friend, Hermione, who is smart and resourceful and helps Harry solve problems with her extreme intelligence. But she still gets relegated to a supporting role and in the end causes trouble with her attractiveness.

There are several problems, for both boys and girls, with a steady diet of the boys-are-heroes message in literature. Boys might learn that the only way to be a successful male is to be a brave, strong, fearless leader. Boys who are sensitive or nurturing, boys whose courage is moral or spiritual rather than physical, might feel that they are not strong or masculine enough. Girls, on the other hand, can develop the notion that it is somehow wrong, not a girl's place, to be a free-willed agent who makes things happen and bravely takes charge of situations.

And what do children learn about friendships between girls and boys when they repeatedly see the boy being the strong protector or the girl as the cute sidekick? What about the boy who needs "rescuing" in some way? Will the girl who thinks she could do it hesitate because it's not part of a girl's job description? Will the boy refuse help because it's not manly to accept it?

What about the girl who is smart, strong, and assertive? Will she learn that she shouldn't speak up? That she can't be an equal part of a friendship with a boy but instead needs to minimize her strengths? These messages lock both boys and girls into narrow roles and hamper children's desires to reach out to one another in healthy ways.

Assess your current reading library

The first step towards balancing the reading library is to take a look at the books you've already got. Pull ten or fifteen books off the shelves at random and look through them. What sort of messages do these books give children about what it means to be a girl or a boy? Masha Rudman, in her book *Children's Literature: An Issues Approach* suggests that to be free of gender bias, books should meet the following criteria:

• Wherever possible, characters should be individuals rather than stereotypes.

• Occupations should, if possible, be gender-free.

• The achievements of both males and females should be judged equally.

• Competition should not be the only way that boys and girls relate.

• Clothing should be consistent with individual personalities and appropriate to activities, etc., rather than gender-determined.

• Whether a character is logical or emotional should be based on the situation rather than on the character's gender.

• Both males and females should be treated with dignity and respect. (Rudman 1995, 181–182)

Evaluating children's books for bias could make an interesting project for students, particularly for older elementary children, who are often acutely aware of what's fair and just. Fifth graders at the Memorial Spaulding School in Newton, Massachusetts, undertook a community service learning project with the goal of helping their peers spot stereotyped media messages and images. They created a pamphlet called *6 Quick Ways for Kids to Analyze Kids' Books for Bias,* which they based on the pamphlet *10 Quick Ways to Analyze Children's Books for Racism and Sexism,* published by the Council on Interracial Books for Children (see Resources section at the end of the book). Written in kid-friendly language, the students' pamphlet asks questions such as:

- In illustrations, is the woman always cooking and the man always hunting? Is the girl always shown playing with dolls?

- Who helps whom? Is it the men who are always helping the women?

- Who are the heroes?

- Who are the victims?

- In cartoons and picture books, are women always doing housework, girls always playing with dolls, and boys playing with cars? (Roberts 2002, 106–107)

If you get children involved in analyzing books for bias, it's important to emphasize that a book that contains stereotyped images is not necessarily a bad book. There are many excellent books that won't pass a gender-equity litmus test. The important thing is that students are aware of potential biases. When you read these books with students, you can offer them a context for approaching the books by talking with them about how girls and boys are portrayed by the author.

For contemporary books, you might ask questions like:

- According to this book, what do boys do? What do girls do?

- How is this like or not like your lives?

- Would the story change if the main character were a boy? A girl?

For older books or books that depict a historical event, you might ask questions like:

- When is the book set?

- When was the book written?

- Who would have been your age at that time? Your parents? Grandparents? Great-grandparents?

- How are things different in the book than they are now?

- What was life like for girls then? Boys then?

Even the ultra-male world of King Arthur and the Round Table can provoke interesting discussions about the rights and responsibilities of medieval royalty, what relationships between men and women were like at that time, or what a modern-day Round Table might look like and what its mission would be. Better yet, read the story of King Arthur along with Robin McKinley's *The Hero and the Crown,* a story about a courageous princess who saves her kingdom by slaying dragons, and compare and contrast the two.

Provide books that show both boys and girls in a variety of roles

You don't need to eliminate all the tales of knights slaying dragons or other boy-hero stories, but it is important to balance them with books that show:

- Girls being heroic

- Boys showing quiet courage

- Girls in active, leader roles, showing resolve, searching for answers

- Boys nurturing others and being emotional

- Boys and girls being caring, brave, and strong

Every year, Deborah Porter reads *The Story of Ruby Bridges* (Coles 1995) with her first grade class. This book tells the story of the six-year-old who was one of the first four African-American children in this country to attend and integrate a white school. Ruby faced angry mobs, police vehicles, and an empty classroom, when she was only in first grade! Porter notes, "When I read that story, I can hear people breathing." For students, the salient point in the Ruby Bridges' story is *she was a little kid. She did a really scary thing.* Her gender matters less than her courage, which sets an example for everyone in the room.

Below is a short list of books that portray boys and girls and men and women in a wide range of roles:

For ages four to eight:

Harriet and the Promised Land written and illustrated by Jacob Lawrence. First published 1968. Paperback edition 1997. New York, NY: Aladdin Library.

A biography of Harriet Tubman, told through paintings and verse.

Oliver Button Is a Sissy written and illustrated by Tomie DePaola. First published 1979. Paperback edition 1990. San Diego, CA: Voyager Books.

Oliver is artistic, likes to read, and attends dancing school. Although he's initially teased by his peers, they eventually support him.

Shoes from Grandpa by Mem Fox. Illustrated by Patricia Mullins. First published 1989. Paperback edition 1992. New York, NY: Orchard Books.

Jesse is an active girl who likes to skateboard. Her family gives her many gifts of clothing but all she wants is jeans.

The Emperor and the Kite by Jane Yolen. Illustrated by Ed Young. First published 1967. Paperback edition 1998. New York, NY: PaperStar Books.

Djeow Seow, the emperor's smallest daughter, uses her kite to rescue her father from a high tower.

The Four Gallant Sisters by Eric A. Kimmel. Illustrated by Tatyana Yuditskaya. 1992. New York, NY: Holt.

In this adaptation of a Grimm fairy tale, four sisters disguise themselves as men in order to learn trades. Eventually, they slay a dragon and rescue four princes, whom they marry. The sisters are valued more for their skill and courage than for their appearance.

William's Doll by Charlotte Zolotow. Illustrated by William Pene du Bois. First published 1972. Paperback edition 1985. New York, NY: Harper Trophy.

When William asks for a doll the men and boys in his life object, but his grandmother gets him a doll.

For ages nine to twelve:

An American Army of Two by Janet Greeson. Illustrated by Patricia Mulvihill. First published 1992. Paperback edition 2003. Minneapolis, MN: First Avenue Editions.

A possibly true story of two young girls who lived in Scituate, Massachusetts, during the war of 1812. They drove off the British army by tricking them into thinking the American army was nearby.

Belva Lockwood Wins Her Case by Drollene Brown. Illustrated by James Watling. 1987. Niles, IL: Albert Whitman & Co.

Biography of the first woman to run for president of the United States and the first to earn the title of doctor of law. Readers get to know her as both real person and hero.

Cut from the Same Cloth: American Women of Myth, Legend, and Tall Tale collected and told by Robert D. San Souci.

Illustrated by Brian Pinkney. First published 1993. Paperback edition 2000. New York, NY: Puffin Books.

A culturally diverse collection of stories about female American folk heroes.

Ernie and the Mile-Long Muffler by Marjorie Lewis. Illustrated by Margo Apple. 1982. New York, NY: Coward, McCann & Geoghehan.

After Uncle Simon teaches Ernie to knit, Ernie decides to knit a mile-long muffler. In the process he learns about arithmetic, friendship, and perseverance.

Girls to the Rescue Series, vols 1 and 2, edited by Bruce Lansky. 1995. Deephaven, MN: Meadowbrook Press.

The two books in the series feature retold fairy tales and original stories from diverse cultures. In all the stories, girls are heroes who, through wits and courage, do things such as saving their village from a tiger, landing a plane in a storm, and saving a gorilla from poachers.

Girls Who Rocked the World: Heroines from Sacagawea to Sheryl Swoopes by Amelie Welden. Illustrations by Jerry McCann. 1998. Hillsboro, OR: Beyond Words Publishing.

Girls Who Rocked the World 2: From Harriet Tubman to Mia Hamm by Michelle Roehm. Illustrations by Jerry McCann. 2000. Milwaukee, WI : Gareth Stevens Publishing.

In this two-book series, the authors profile women who achieved great things before the age of twenty. The book also includes responses from modern girls to the question: How will you rock the world?

Justin and the Best Biscuits in the World by Mildred Walter. Illustrated by Catherine Stock. First published 1986. Paperback edition 2000. New York, NY: Dell Yearling.

When ten-year-old Justin visits his grandfather's ranch, he learns to do ranch work. But he also learns how to cook and clean, work that the grandfather calls "human work" rather than "woman's work."

Shiloh by Phyllis Reynolds Naylor. Paperback edition illustrated by Barry Moser. First published 1991. Paperback edition 2000. New York, NY: Aladdin Paperbacks.

> In a story that raises complex ethical issues, eleven-year-old Marty rescues a dog from an abusive owner.

The Midnight Fox by Betsy Cromer Byars. Illustrated by Ann Grifalconi. First published 1968. Paperback edition 2001. New York, NY: Puffin Books.

> Tommy spends the summer on a farm. While there, he observes and then nurtures a fox and her baby.

Provide books that show girls and boys in healthy friendships

There's an abundance of children's books portraying either antagonistic relationships between boys and girls or strong same-gender friendships. Scarcer are books that show strong and loyal friendships between boys and girls. Below is a short list of books about boy-girl friendships:

Ages four to eight:

Chester's Way by Kevin Henkes. First published 1988. Paperback edition 1997. New York, NY: Mulberry Books.

> Two best friends, Chester and Wilson, become three best friends when Lilly moves in.

Chicken Sunday by Patricia Polacco. First published 1992. Paperback edition 1998. New York, NY: PaperStar Books.

> Friends Winnie, Stewart, and Winston earn money for an Easter hat for Gramma and in the process befriend an old man.

Child of Faerie, Child of Earth by Jane Yolen. Illustrated by Jane Dyer. First published 1997. Paperback edition 2000. Boston, MA: Little, Brown.

> The story of a human girl and a fairy boy who are lifelong friends despite their differences.

Iris and Walter by Elissa Haden Guest. Illustrated by Christine Davenier. First published 2000. Paperback edition 2002. New York, NY; San Diego, CA: Gulliver Books.

Iris is very unhappy when her family moves from the city to the country. But then she meets a new friend, Walter, and begins to enjoy herself.

Wings written and illustrated by Christopher Myers. 2000. New York, NY: Scholastic Press.

Ikarus Jackson can fly. At first the townspeople are in awe but eventually they taunt him. One girl, however, speaks up for him.

Ages nine to twelve:

Amber Brown Is Not a Crayon by Paula Danziger. Illustrated by Tony Ross. First published 1994. Paperback edition 1995. New York, NY: Scholastic.

Third graders Amber and Justin have been friends for a long time. When Justin announces that his family is moving away, Amber's first response is to fight with Justin but they eventually make up.

Bridge to Terabithia by Katherine Paterson. Illustrated by Donna Diamond. 1977. Paperback edition 2003. New York, NY: Harper Trophy.

A wonderful friendship grows between country boy Jess and city girl Leslie. Leslie transforms Jess's life before she tragically drowns.

December Secrets by Patricia Reilly Giff. Illustrated by Blanche Sims. 1984. New York, NY: Yearling Books.

Emily Arrow and Richard Best are best friends who depend on each other.

The Facts and Fictions of Minna Pratt by Patricia MacLachlan. First published 1988. Paperback edition 2002. New York, NY: HarperTrophy.

Minna discovers important truths about herself and her family through her friendship with Lucas Ellerby.

The Merchant of Marvels and the Peddlar of Dreams by Frederic Clement, translated by Emma Cole. 1997. San Francisco, CA: Chronicle Books.

Frederick Knick-Knack looks for the perfect gift for his friend Alice, a girl who has everything.

Words of Stone by Kevin Henkes. First published 1992. Paperback edition 1993. New York, NY: Puffin Books.

Eleven-year-old Blaze becomes friends with Joselle but then discovers that Joselle once did something to hurt him. A suspenseful story that looks at issues of friendship, conflict, betrayal, and reconciliation.

Help children become critical readers

A balanced reading library can offer boys and girls a different vision of themselves and of what's possible in their relationships with each other. However, it's important not to use books simply to teach lessons about gender equity. Instead, provide interesting, well-written books that capture children's imaginations, deepen their knowledge of self, and broaden their world. As you read and discuss a wide range of books with children, the children will become more critical readers who can make their own informed choices about books.

Activity

"The New Dick and Jane: Gender Stereotypes and Children's Literature," lesson plan available online from *Gender Equity Lesson Plans and Teacher Guide* (http://www.genderequity.org/book/lesson21.html)

Students review young children's books for gender bias and then rewrite biased material in a more balanced way. Although designed for use with high school students, this lesson plan could be adapted for use with upper elementary students.

Works Cited

Coles, Robert. 1995. *The Story of Ruby Bridges.* Illustrated by George Ford. New York, NY: Scholastic.

Roberts, Pamela. 2002. *Kids Taking Action: Community Service Learning Projects, K–8.* Greenfield, MA: Northeast Foundation for Children.

Rudman, Masha. 1995. *Children's Literature: An Issues Approach.* 3rd edition. White Plains, NY: Longman Publishers.

Strategy Seven: Find Ways to Supplement Textbooks

THE SECOND GRADERS *in Mr. Roseman's room are excited about their social studies unit because they get to study the local community. They go on tours of local businesses and organizations and interesting guests come into the classroom to talk with them. Earlier this week a woman police officer came to the school and brought her horse! The students eagerly gathered outside where they got to touch the horse and ask the police officer lots of questions.*

In Ms. Patenaude's sixth grade class, the students are doing an Internet research project gathering information for a class book called "Unsung Heroes of Science." They've discovered all sorts of people who made discoveries or inventions, including lots of women, such as chemist Rosalind Franklin, who was the first person to recognize the helix shape of DNA.

We've come a long way from the time when the curriculum routinely showed stereotyped images of men and women. Many of us remember, for instance, the days when *Fun with Dick and Jane*—the '50s era adventures of a Caucasian, middle-class family, with Mommy baking cookies and Daddy smoking his pipe—dominated the reading shelves in elementary school classrooms.

In newer textbooks, particularly language arts, science, and math texts, girls and boys and men and women of different ethnic groups are seen working and playing side by side, in comparable roles. Unfortunately, many financially strapped school systems need to use old textbooks, which often are filled with images of men and women in stereotyped roles. And even in new texts there are gaps.

Heath, Massachusetts, elementary teacher Deborah Porter describes her state's mandated history curriculum as "Great White Male History." Many teachers, both male and female, feel the same way. Boston teacher Gail Zimmerman says with a sigh,

"We start in first grade with the awareness that we're beginning twelve years of the study of history, and that there will be an enormous bias."

Here's one small illustration of this kind of bias:

Ethlie Ann Vare and Greg Ptacek, in their book *Mothers of Invention* recount the story of Catherine Littlefield Greene, the widow of a Revolutionary War general. Eli Whitney lived on her estate while he perfected his design for the cotton gin. Whitney, repeatedly frustrated with his early designs because cottonseeds clogged up the rollers, used Greene's idea to incorporate brushes for the seeds. This design succeeded. But legally, women were not allowed to hold patents. Because Greene's name does not appear with Whitney's on the patent, despite their collaboration and her substantial financial contribution, the credit, the immediate fame, and the place in history are his. The "official story" of Eli Whitney told in history books boils down to: Eli Whitney, inventor of the cotton gin instead of the story of a man and woman's shoulder-to-shoulder struggle and friendship. (Sadker and Sadker 1994, 67)

To better understand the impact that such a lopsided curriculum could have on students and on relationships between boys and girls, consider the following allegory. Imagine for a moment a group of blue and green fourth graders. Day after day, week after week, year after year, they learn about the history of the blue people. Everyone is familiar with the names of blue heroes. Every piece of paper was signed, every war was fought, every treaty was negotiated by someone blue. Both blue and green children are assigned to write reports about famous blues. Every holiday that results in a long weekend commemorates someone blue. Every time the students buy something, all the paper money and most of the coins they use are adorned with the faces of blues.

Greens, however, are rarely mentioned. It is as if they never existed. Why should anybody care about them? What can greens possibly say or do that would be interesting or valuable? Why should blues value friendships and working relationships with greens? This little allegory, obvious though it is, illustrates how teaching a lopsided curriculum could affect students' beliefs about what is possible for both genders and about how the two can relate to one another.

Give children a balanced view of men's and women's contributions

The first step in moving towards a more balanced curriculum is to review the texts you use in all subject areas. Here are some questions to ask yourself:

• In science and math texts, are there images of women as well as men conducting experiments, using computers, discovering stars, exploring space, solving problems?

• In science and math texts, are there images of men and women working together?

• Do science and math texts discuss both male and female inventors, physicists, chemists, engineers, mathematicians?

• In literature texts, are both males and females the protagonists in stories?

• In social studies texts, are there images of both men and women in a variety of roles?

• In social studies texts, are there discussions of both male and female explorers, settlers, pioneers, revolutionaries, leaders, peacemakers?

Chances are that you'll find men represented more often than women in textbooks, particularly in older texts. This doesn't mean you should discard the texts—or sidestep the mandated curricula that the texts support; instead, think about ways you can supplement the texts and work within the curriculum to give children a view of both men and women creating, building, dreaming, struggling, and discovering.

When Deborah Porter teaches first graders about heroes, for instance, she makes sure to include such figures as Harriet Tubman and Ruby Bridges (both female *and* African-American). Likewise, Gail Zimmerman includes females such as Pocahontas and Sacagawea when her second and third grade classes study Native Americans and explorers.

Studies of the community offer a valuable opportunity to shine the spotlight on women and men in a wide variety of roles.

When Deborah Porter's class studies the school community as part of a social studies unit, they build a model of the school and then talk about who does what. Does the principal have to be a man? she asks. Does the school nurse have to be a woman? At her school, there are lots of models of men and women who defy stereotypes. A classroom aide, whom all the kids adore, is a female carpenter. A sixth grade teacher is a man. Porter uses these opportunities to help students broaden their vision of what's possible for girls and boys.

Porter also invites community members into her classroom. She brings in women doctors and lawyers, families where both parents work together running a farm or a business, women police officers. "The greatest program ever," Porter says, "was a visit from Cady Coleman, an astronaut. She's this tiny woman, not particularly muscular. She brought slides and her spacesuit and talked to the kids about how she became an astronaut."

At the Jackson Mann school in Boston, teachers of older grades have developed a unit of study to teach children about the important role of women in Massachusetts and Boston history. Gail Zimmerman, who teaches younger children at Jackson Mann, admires the work these teachers have done to create a relevant, region-specific unit—and the inspiration the unit provides for the Jackson Mann students. "These women, many of whom

were African-American, achieved against incredible odds, with two strikes against them: they were women and they were Black. They were not expected to, or supposed to, succeed."

Below are some suggestions and resources for creating a more gender-inclusive curriculum:

- In a unit on heroes, work with students to define the various forms that heroism can take and then ask students to write stories about heroes, male and female, that they know in their everyday lives.

- Help students see historical events through multiple perspectives. One way to do this is to develop a cooperative learning project. Divide students into small groups and assign each student in a group a point-of-view through which they investigate the event. For example, in a unit on the American Revolution, one student could be a colonist, another could be a British soldier, another could be a female shopkeeper, another could be a Native American. One place to get information about designing projects like this is through the San Diego State University WebQuest website, http://webquest.sdsu.edu/webquest.html

- Use Internet resources to access materials about women inventors, historical figures, scientists, and mathematicians. Some good websites are:

  National Women's History Project (www.nwhp.org)

  Association for Women in Mathematics (www.awm-math.org/biographies.html)

  Women of NASA (http://quest.arc.nasa.gov/women/intro.html)

  4000 Years of Women in Science (www.astr.ua.edu/4000WS/ 4000WS.html)

Work Cited

Sadker, David, and Myra Sadker. 1994. *Failing at Fairness: How Our Schools Cheat Girls*. New York, NY: Simon and Schuster.

Strategy Eight: Pay Attention to What's on the Walls and Shelves

E VERY DECISION A TEACHER MAKES in the classroom, including what displays to put up and what materials to provide, has an impact on how boys and girls view themselves and each other. Although the impact might be less direct than decisions about lining up, grouping, seating, and class discussions, choices about classroom displays and materials still influence gender relationships.

Create displays that reinforce cohesion rather than separation

Displaying student work in the classroom can be a wonderful way to build a sense of community and to help children feel known and valued as individuals. Many teachers start the year with little displayed on the classroom walls, leaving plenty of room for student work. Fourth grade teacher Jane Stephenson notes, "The only thing on my walls not done by students is the calendar."

If you do display students' work in the classroom, it's important to make sure that girls' and boys' work is equally represented and that boys and girls are equally involved in helping to create the displays. Following are a few suggestions for achieving balanced displays of student work:

- Make sure there is always at least one display that includes work from every child in the class. Avoid putting grades or teacher's notes on student work that is displayed.

- Display student work that results from an assignment where all children are illustrating the same topic. For example, as part of a science lesson, children might draw leaves, flowers, insects, etc. A display of twenty-five different drawings of the same insect highlights and celebrates individual differences within the context of a cohesive group—and sidesteps the possibility of gender-typed drawings.

- At the beginning of the year, create a colorful display that names and illustrates each child's hopes for the year. This can be left up all year long as a reminder of the importance of each individual within the classroom community.

- Invite students to work together on creating displays. Better yet, create girl-boy pairings and assign them the job of creating and maintaining a particular display.

For teachers who use store-bought materials to create displays, here are some things to pay attention to:

- Be sure that boys and men are shown in a wide range of roles, including helping and nurturing roles.

- Be sure that girls and women are shown in a wide range of roles, including active, decisive, or technical roles.

- Display posters that show boys and girls and men and women working together as equal partners.

- Think about where you put the posters or other images. For example, you might want to put images of women building things in the blocks area or images of men cooking or cleaning in the kitchen area.

In primary grades, stock the shelves with materials that nourish imagination and promote common play

How many times have you walked into a toy store and noticed the sharp division between the so-called "girls" and "boys" aisles? While there's no official sign marking the aisles, everyone knows that the ones filled with purple and pink toys are for the girls, the ones with black and green toys for the boys. Even more differentiated is the content of the toys. For girls, there's an abundance of items related to the home or personal adornment: baby dolls and strollers, oven sets, and glittery jewelry kits. For boys, there are walkie-talkies, every make of vehicle, and an endless variety of toy weapons. Even Nerf, known for its "soft toys," now produces an enormous machine gun-type weapon that rapidly shoots foam darts.

By the time most children enter kindergarten, they have spent several years defining their play by the merchandise foisted upon them. Often this results in a limited choice of activities and play partners. Predictably, girls will gravitate to other girls for play involving housekeeping and animal or people care, while boys will gravitate to other boys for play involving adventure and fighting.

Fortunately, primary grade children are still very receptive to broadening their play horizons. Teachers can help them do this, particularly by providing a rich assortment of materials for imaginative play and guidance on how to use these materials. Inspired by recommendations made by Nancy Carlsson-Paige and Diane E. Levin in *Who's Calling the Shots? How to Respond Effectively to Children's Fascination with War Play and War Toys and Violent TV!*, K–1 teacher Susan Pelis decided to collect interesting materials for students to use during outside playtime for imaginative, dramatic free play. She began by asking families for help. The results were positive:

> Parents brought in old suitcases, old lunchboxes, rope, tires, wooden blocks, crates, a laundry basket, etc. That year I had some boys who were very rough and tumble, physical kids. Often their play was aggressive. I grouped them with some girls who usually shied away from physical play. Together

they used these materials to create a wonderful "kitty ship." It was playful, rich with language experiences, very inclusive, imaginative, and completely nonviolent.

Carlsson-Paige and Levin list many items that lend themselves to imaginative and collaborative play. For example:

- A section of an old tree can be a stage or a table.

- Large appliance cartons can be caves, houses, hideouts.

- Telephones are great for imaginary conversations.

- Oars and paddles lead to sea adventures.

- Plastic laundry baskets can be ships, canoes, beds, or even birds' nests.

- Tubes (cardboard, plastic) make great walkie-talkies or megaphones.

- Buttons make great coins, pirate treasure, jewelry.

- Old jewelry, eyeglasses without lenses, clothes, hats, scarves are useful for costumes. (Carlsson-Paige and Levin 1990)

Once you've collected an array of props, explore with the children the possibilities for their use. Begin by brainstorming ideas for what students might do with the various materials. Asking the class questions such as, "What are twenty different things we could do with this box?" will provide a rich array of ideas. Depending on the class, you might want to assign children to groups to ensure a balance of gender, interests, and abilities. And you'll want to supervise the groups closely, supporting cooperative friendly play and discouraging aggressive play that might become hurtful.

Work Cited

Carlsson-Paige, Nancy, and Diane E. Levin. 1990. *Who's Calling the Shots? How to Respond Effectively to Children's Fascination with War Play and War Toys and Violent TV!* Gabriola Island, BC: New Society Publishers.

Outside the Classroom

Strategy Nine:
Structure Lunch to Bring Boys and Girls Together

Strategy Ten:
Provide Opportunities for Girls and Boys to Play Together Safely at Recess

NO MATTER how much energy, time, and thought a teacher puts into improving relationships between boys and girls in the classroom, it can all fall apart in the lunchroom and on the playground if there's a lack of structure and low expectations for behavior in these areas. And as every teacher knows, the resulting angry or hurt feelings can easily spill over into the classroom, undermining the work that the teacher and children have done to build positive relationships between girls and boys.

It's easiest to achieve change outside the classroom if there's a school-wide effort to create and sustain a positive social climate. But even one teacher working towards change can have an impact on children's experiences at lunch and recess. Strategy nine offers ideas for creating a safe framework for lunch and suggests ways of structuring lunch that will bring boys and girls together. Strategy ten focuses on improving relationships between girls and boys on the playground.

Strategy Nine: Structure Lunch to Bring Boys and Girls Together

I<small>T'S EARLY</small> D<small>ECEMBER</small> *and Mr. Thomas's efforts to bridge the gender gap in his fifth grade classroom seem to be working. The students enjoy opportunities to work in mixed-gender groups and no longer need prompting to seek out new partners at choice time. All the students are thriving in this environment. Even shy, isolated Jake, who at the beginning of the year couldn't introduce himself during Morning Meeting, is now sought after as a partner at choice time. Students have come to know Jake and to value his sense of humor and artistic ability.*

But at lunch it's different. Mr. Thomas sees students splitting off into exclusive groups for lunch—usually all-boy and all-girl— with a few students, such as Jake, straggling off by themselves. And judging by the conversations he hears as the students return from lunch, there's bullying and teasing going on in the lunchroom. Mr. Thomas wants to help the children do lunch differently. He decides to begin by talking with them about how their classroom rules can apply to the lunchroom.

Create a safe framework for lunch

Although some of the factors affecting the social climate of the lunchroom are beyond the classroom teacher's influence, there are steps a teacher can take to improve the lunchroom experience. For example, asking students to describe what their classroom rules would look like and sound like in the lunchroom can help students apply these rules to lunchroom behavior.

Another approach is to establish lunchroom rules in the same way that you establish classroom rules: talk with students about their goals for lunch and then help them create rules that will allow them to reach those goals. Just as with classroom rules, students will be far more invested in following rules that they helped create and that help them achieve their goals.

For instance, in opening a conversation with a third grade class about lunch, a teacher begins by asking students what they hope for at lunch:

- "To talk with my friends," offers one student.

- "To have fun."

- "To have enough time to eat my whole lunch."

- "To relax and have a break from doing so much work."

After listening to their responses, the teacher summarizes, "So your goals for lunchtime are to have a fun and relaxing break, to be able to talk with friends, and to eat your lunch. What rules can you think of that would help you all do this?"

Students will typically begin this process by generating rules about what they shouldn't do:

- Don't yell.

- Don't be mean to people.

- Don't run around.

Teachers can help them reframe these in the positive by reminding students to keep the focus on what they *should* do, rather than on what they *shouldn't* do. Here is a partial list of the third graders' lunchtime rules:

- Talk in soft voices.

- Stay at your table until the bell rings.

- Be nice to the people working in the cafeteria.

- Be friendly and let anyone sit at your table.

- Remember to eat your lunch.

- Be respectful of people's food preferences.

Students can write the rules on a poster, which gets hung by the classroom door or even in the lunchroom. If lunchroom rules or general school rules already exist, the teacher might want to share these rules with students and ask them to comment on how they compare to the list the students generated.

Once rules are established, the next step is to model and practice good lunchroom behavior: talking quietly, acting in a friendly manner towards other students and staff, making a minimal mess, staying in your seat, cleaning up your tray, etc. It is particularly helpful to discuss what to do when a student from another class, who might not be paying attention to the same rules, behaves in a disruptive way. Teachers can model what it might look like to simply ignore the behavior, to ask the child to stop, or to get help from an adult if the situation feels out of control.

Finally, before lunch on the next day, the teacher might remind students of the guidelines they've created and let them know that she'll be checking in with them after lunch to see how things went. These debriefing sessions can be short and sweet. Every few days, the teacher can briefly check in with students by asking questions such as, "How did lunch go today?" "Which rules were easy to follow?" "Which ones were hard?" "Any ideas for making lunch more enjoyable?"

Set up structures for inviting someone new to lunch

Ms. Robley decided to address the lunch problem at the beginning of the year. During the first month of school, the students in her grade three-four class became familiar with the routines of lunch, they established rules for the lunchroom, and they practiced living those rules. Now, at the end of September, she's introducing a new routine called "lunch inviting." The idea, she reminds the class, is to eat lunch with a variety of people, not just the same friends every day. However, inviting someone different to lunch is not a gesture that comes naturally—to adults or children—so she opens up a discussion:

Ms. Robley: Why do you think it might be a good idea to have different lunch partners?

Tina: So you don't have to eat lunch by yourself.

Meredith (giggling): So you can see what other people have in their lunch box.

Rob: So you won't get bored eating with the same people all the time. Maybe you can get to know someone new.

Ms. Robley responds, "All those are great reasons. And remember that we've been working on boys and girls getting along and feeling comfortable with each other. Talking to each other at lunch is another opportunity for you get to know each other better."

The earlier in the year you can introduce the routine of lunch inviting the better. Let students become comfortable with the routines of lunch; establish rules for lunch; teach, model, and practice good lunch behavior—and then introduce lunch inviting. Begin with a discussion of the goals for lunch inviting (for example, getting to know new people, or boys and girls talking together). Be sure that students understand that improving gender relationships is as important at lunch as it is in the classroom.

Once you know that students understand the goals of eating lunch with a variety of classmates, it's time to discuss the logistics. Here are two key areas to address:

• Model how to invite someone to be a lunch partner and how to graciously accept an invitation. In many classrooms, teachers establish a rule that the only time students can turn down an invitation is when they already have a lunch partner.

• Talk about students' responsibilities to one another as friendly classmates and lunch partners: How do the classroom rules apply to lunch inviting? How do I respond if someone I don't like invites me to lunch? What does it mean to be friendly even with people who aren't your good friends?

When the children are ready, set aside one or two days a week that are "new friend" lunch days. A good way to facilitate choosing partners is to post a lunch chart on the wall. Down one side list each child's name. Next to the name put a Velcro backed tag that also has the child's name. First thing in the morning on each "new friend" day, children choose a lunch partner by looking at the chart to see who doesn't have a partner yet and inviting one of those people to lunch. Then the two children go together to the chart and place their names next to one another.

Encourage students to choose a variety of partners and on some days to choose a partner of the opposite gender. You can structure the process by asking students to choose a partner based on a category that you name—for example, "Invite a student who's wearing the same color shirt as you," or "Invite someone who has read a book that you also read." Children tend to like these "category invitations," and with a little care in devising categories, you can ensure that children who are not often chosen for teams or groups are likely to get invited first. Here are some other ways to prevent students from only choosing favorite classmates:

• Make a rule that students have to invite the first person they come across who fits the category.

• Set a time challenge: Students must find a partner who fits the category in less than ten seconds, for example.

• Require students to invite someone they haven't had lunch with in the past two weeks.

After a bit more practice, let students come up with the categories. They can get very absorbed in inventing odd categories, which helps pull their attention away from trying to invite certain classmates and not others. Whether you come up with the categories or the students do, make sure the categories change often as a way to shuffle the friendship deck.

Below are two additional ideas for partnering children for lunch so that students have the chance to eat with a wide range of classmates:

Assigning lunch partners

The simplest way is to pair children randomly. But you can also pair them based on a commonality—for example, the two children have the same initials, same number of letters in their names, or the same birthday month. The two children can try to guess what their "commonality" is, which adds fun, gives the children a conversation starter, and helps them get to know each other. Or you could form small groups based on your knowledge of common interests or traits and then have students guess the commonality.

Drawing names to form pairs

Many teachers write students' names on Popsicle sticks, one name per stick. Students draw sticks to see who their partner will be that day. Each day, change the order in which students draw, so that different students have a chance to draw first. For example, one day you can go in reverse alphabetical order by last name, another day you can go around a circle, yet another day you can go by students' birth date order.

After lunch on "new friend" days, have a brief class meeting to talk about what happened at lunch. What went well? What was hard? You can also give students tasks to complete during lunch that they then report back on, such as discovering one area of common interest.

Finally, be careful not to over-use partner lunches. It's a good idea to intersperse lunch partner days with "open" days when children can eat with anyone they'd like. It's important to give children opportunities both to practice friendliness with every-one and to deepen their bonds with their close friends.

Teach students how to have good lunch conversations

Part of the reason it can be uncomfortable to meet new people is that it's sometimes hard to know what to talk about: How do you find out about common interests? What if there's a long silence? What if you disagree about something? Who talks first?

90

You can make "new friend" lunches easier by directly addressing the topic of lunch conversations. If you do a *Responsive Classroom*® Morning Meeting, then the skills that children learn during the sharing component will help make lunch conversations easier. During sharing, students learn to speak clearly, stay focused on a topic, ask questions that are open-ended and relevant, and make empathic comments. As preparation for inviting someone new to lunch, remind students of these skills that they already know and practice daily. Ask children, "How can you use these skills to have a conversation with someone you don't know very well?"

For any group, including groups that don't have a regular sharing routine, ask questions such as:

• Why do we have conversations with friends and classmates?

• What makes conversation between people interesting?

• What kinds of questions encourage people to tell us more about something?

• How can we tell that someone is listening carefully?

• In a good conversation, what's the responsibility of the speaker? Of the listener?

From this discussion, students should be able to make a list of "successful conversation ingredients" which can be posted in the classroom and referred to as students work on developing their conversation skills. Items on the list might include:

• Look at the person who's talking.

• Listen carefully.

• Ask relevant questions.

• Speak clearly.

• Give everyone a chance to talk.

Next, model having a conversation, then ask students to practice. If you'd like to give some structure to these practice sessions, you can suggest a beginning question, such as, "What do you like to do after school?" Before partnering up to practice, students could brainstorm a series of questions that could keep the conversation going:

• Where do you usually do the activity?

• Why do you like it?

• Tell me more about...

To encourage careful listening, ask students to report back on what they learned from their partners.

Finally, ask the class to brainstorm a list of interesting, fun topics for their lunchtime conversations. Topics might include:

• Favorite (weekend, summer, winter) activities

• Favorite (sports or games, books or movies)

• A place I like to be

• The people and pets in my family

• Collections

• Favorite books or movies

• Something funny that happened to me

Once you have a good list of topics, you could write the topics on separate index cards and put them all into a box. Individual students can draw topics from the box as they set off to lunch or you can draw a topic that becomes the "topic of the week." For follow-up, you can ask students to report back on their lunchtime conversations during the "after-lunch" meeting. You could also pool the results of a lunchtime conversation and create an exhibit for the lunchroom—"What We Learned about Each Other."

Finally, a simple but powerful strategy to help build positive relationships between boys and girls is to teach children some fun and appropriate games that they can play while waiting for lunch to be done. Brainstorm a list, make sure everyone knows how to play, post the list, and then each day before leaving the classroom remind children to pick a game that they will use if necessary. There are a few ideas on the following pages to help you and your students get started.

Activities

Alphabet Story

The first person in the circle starts to tell a story with a sentence beginning with the letter "A" ("Aunt Helen came to my house the other day," for example). The next person in the circle continues, adding a sentence that begins with "B" ("Buddy, her terrier, came with her"). The class continues through the alphabet until everyone has added to the story.

Aunt Minerva

The child who begins the activity decides on a category such as "hot" but does not tell anyone else. Instead s/he gives several examples to demonstrate the category by telling things that Aunt Minerva likes and doesn't like. For example, if the category is "hot," s/he might say, "Aunt Minerva likes Florida but doesn't like Alaska. Aunt Minerva likes heavy down quilts but doesn't like thin sheets. Aunt Minerva likes soup but doesn't like ice cream." The other players try to figure out the category. When they know the category, they give an example of something Aunt Minerva likes and doesn't like. The child who began the activity acknowledges whether the guesser is right or not. The leader keeps giving examples and listening to others' guesses until many of the children have the category.

To keep this activity from feeling frustrating, end one round and begin another before there are only a handful of children still guessing.

Fact or Fiction

A student tells three things about him/herself—two facts and one fiction. For example, the student might say, "I've been to France. I play the tuba. I've got three cats." Going around the circle, everyone makes a guess about which claim is fiction. The student then says which students guessed correctly, and someone else takes a turn.

Guess the Number

Think of a number and write it down on a piece of paper that you hide. Let students know that you've chosen a number between one and ____, choosing a number range that appropriately challenges the group, given their age and skill level. Going around the circle, students take turns asking a yes-or-no question to try to determine the number. Encourage students to think of questions that will give them information about the number, rather than questions that just eliminate one number. Instead of asking if it's the number after fourteen, for example, students might ask if it's a two-digit number, whether it's larger than ten, or if it has a five in it.

If a student does not have a question, s/he may "pass." A student who thinks s/he knows the number may take a guess. If the guess is incorrect, the questioning continues. If it's correct, the teacher may choose another number or pick a child to choose a number. To emphasize the cooperative nature of this activity, be sure that the child who correctly guesses the number is not the next one to choose a number. The ultimate goal of this activity is to see how many numbers the group can figure out within a certain period of time.

I Spy

One person says "I spy with my little eye, something that is (color)". Then others try to guess what the object is and the one who guesses it takes the next turn.

Rock, Paper, Scissors

In pairs, children begin with an agreed on count-in (emphasize use of quiet voices), such as, "1-2-3-Go!" On the word "Go," the two children each show a hand symbol. Children choose from the symbol for rock (a fist), paper (an open hand), or scissors (index and middle finger extended). Each symbol can beat and be beaten by another symbol: rock crushes scissors; scissors cut paper; paper covers rock.

Strategy Ten: Provide Opportunities for Girls and Boys to Play Together Safely at Recess

Nowhere is the separation of boys and girls more pronounced than on the school playground. Here's a typical scene:

> Boys blanket the fields and courts, playing team sports such as soccer or basketball. Girls cluster in the smaller spaces close to the building, talking, climbing on bars, or jumping rope. Boys may wander over to the girls but be rebuffed by the girls who tell them to "Leave us alone!" Girls interested in sports may attempt to join the boys' games, only to be told, "No girls allowed!" Chasing or "catch and kiss" games may develop, which appear to represent integrated play, but are based on gender antagonism and opposition, not integration. (Thorne 1993, 44)

Often, whether a child gets included in active games or left out depends on athletic skill. In a very public, witnessed arena, those who have athletic skill are chosen first for teams; those who don't are chosen last or left on the sidelines. As students grow older, and competition becomes more and more important for the athletically skilled, the range of acceptable ability for spontaneously chosen teams narrows. Unfortunately, this narrowing squeezes out most girls. Physical education teacher Mark Farnsworth describes the situation this way:

> An intense desire to separate begins in second or third grade, especially in physical education and at recess. Boys really start to assert themselves. They want to play hard and win. The girls wonder why the boys are so competitive, and why they don't want to include girls. I think that's a very difficult time for the girls.

This separation based on ability and competition occurs against a backdrop of a simple difference in focus. Watch a group of boys run onto the playground and it's likely that many of them will head straight to the playing fields, form teams, choose balls, and start playing a competitive sport. Girls, by contrast, will typically pay less attention to games that require speed and competition and more to feats of dexterity. They're more likely to gravitate toward jump rope, hopscotch, jacks, and monkey bar climbing, all of which require individual skill at complicated physical maneuvers.

In this setting, some bold children will attempt to cross the heavily policed gender boundaries, but most won't. Those who do try do so at the risk of being teased. (Thorne 1993, 125) Because few girls or boys are confident enough to cross the playground gender line, it is up to teachers and administrators to make the playground a safe place to come together and try something new.

As with making changes in lunchroom behavior, change on the playground is easiest when approached as a school-wide effort, with the support of administrators and the collaboration of other teachers and aides. Many schools focus attention on "teaching" recess, just as they teach math or reading. But even if you are alone in your desire to improve recess or are one of a small group of teachers, there are things you can do that will make recess a safer and friendlier environment, where boys and girls can play together. And maybe as other teachers and administrators see children playing together cooperatively and safely, they'll become interested in the changes you've begun.

Teach and lead structured play

Ms. Gronowski, a second grade teacher, used to dread recess. All too often the students would return from the playground angry and upset. But this year she and the other two second grade teachers decided to structure recess. Early in the year, they talked with the students about "rules for recess" that were extensions of the classroom rules. Then they and the students brainstormed a long list of recess activities, some quiet and some active, that could provide something for everyone to do. Each day the children choose from three activities. Today's choices are swinging, hopscotch, and kickball. Ms. Gronowski and two aides will be present to supervise the activities—and to join in the fun!

Teaching and leading more structured play at recess can prevent the gender separation that almost invariably occurs in unstructured, "open" recess. Following are some ideas for "teaching recess":

Early in the year, take students on an exploration of the playground.

Include the equipment that's available during recess. Younger students might need to learn how to use the equipment. With older students, you can have a conversation in which you review safe ways to use the equipment and brainstorm games that can be played with different pieces of equipment.

Talk about how classroom rules apply to recess.

For example, what does it mean to take care of each other on the playground? What does it look like to be in control of yourself when you're playing kickball? What does it sound like to be friendly when someone asks to join a game?

Ask students what special rules are needed to make recess safe and fun for all.

These rules might include guidelines for how to join a game, how to include one another in games, and how to take turns.

Work with the principal and recess teachers to structure recess as a set of choices.

For example, every day, students might choose from a variety of activities, all of which are led or supervised by an adult. Choices could include jump rope, climbing structure, Capture the Flag, drawing with chalk, kickball, etc.

Structure games that are easy to enter and that accommodate different skill levels.

In observing children's playground interactions at different schools, sociologist Barrie Thorne noticed that games such as handball, which simply requires that a new player get in line behind others who are waiting, or kickball, which does not demand a high level of gross-motor coordination, were popular with both genders. (Thorne 1993, 54) In general, games that are open to all players and that have a simple and easy-to-understand process for admitting new players, have the best likelihood of gender integration.

Teach girls new skills

When boys are engaged in organized competition on the playing fields and girls are hanging out by the doorway talking, the reason may have less to do with segregation and more with ignorance. Girls may simply not know any physical games to play, or feel awkward about playing them. Many teachers report success in working alone with girls, teaching them how to play team sports. Although this may seem like a strategy that promotes segregation rather than integration, learning how to play a sport with other girls can give girls a greater sense of legitimacy and purpose on the playground. It can also help them gain confidence in physical skills so they feel comfortable playing in mixed-gender groups.

One classroom teacher spent many recesses teaching a group of girls to play foursquare. Another teacher asked a group of girls what sport they wanted to learn and then started a girls volleyball team. Ruth Sidney Charney had great eventual success teaching a group of girls to play kickball. She notes:

> One year, there was a group of boys who went on to become sports stars, some of the best soccer players in the county. During outdoor breaks, the boys played intense games of soccer, foursquare, and basketball, while the girls wandered aimlessly around the playground. I, who am not particularly athletic, went onto the fields with the girls and required them to play kickball. They played three days a week, and my rule was that they couldn't whine too much. They could whine for maybe two minutes and then had to go out and take their positions. After a few weeks, we began having the most wonderful time. They got so serious about it. The girls began to play on their free time, to practice throwing, catching, running. When they were given their own arena, they were able to do sports, wanted to do them, took a lot of pride in how well they could do them.

Having these arenas open up to them emboldened the girls to participate more in other activities. The girls made their presence felt on the playing fields and began to command more respect from boys, an indirect step towards integration.

A more direct way to respond to sports inequity and to bring boys and girls together is to teach all children a new sport, one that requires a different set of skills from the usual sports of baseball, basketball, or soccer. Sports such as ultimate Frisbee or games such as Capture the Flag, for example, require coordination, cooperation, and strategy more than speed or strength. This can level the field for girls and boys, and provide equal fun and challenge to both genders.

Teach cooperative games

Children subjected to daily competitive schoolyard contests are constantly driven from playing fields, in greater and greater numbers as they grow older. Terry Orlick, a leading figure in the cooperative sports movement, writes:

> Pitting children against one another in games where they frantically compete for what only a few can have guarantees failure and rejection for the many. Many children's games and programs are in fact designed for elimination. Many ensure that one wins and everyone else loses, leaving sport "rejects" and "dropouts" to form the vast majority of our North American population. (Orlick 1978, 5)

Children who experience failure and rejection in competitive sports develop a lower self-esteem and body image overall, according to Orlick. This is bad for boys, whose culture demands that they keep on playing, in spite of the risk of failure, and for girls, whose self-esteem and body image begin to lurch precariously during the middle grades. (Orlick 1978, 6)

Physical education teacher Mark Farnsworth is an enthusiastic proponent of playing cooperative sports during recess. Games from other cultures, modified games of "ball," ungames, and hybrids all de-emphasize the athletic ability pecking order and focus on cooperation, acceptance of others, involvement, and fun. (Orlick 1978, 7) In the Resources section at the end of the book, you'll find a list of recommended resources for these kinds of games. Because the pressure to win is taken away, children can simply enjoy playing; they are released from the fear of making a mistake and can instead learn from mistakes.

Below are some fun games that emphasize movement and teamwork over winning and are ideal for playing with mixed-gender groups during recess.

Tag the Leader *(from first grade teacher Maureen Russell)*

A student in the middle of the circle (the leader) throws up a ball, and the other children run in to try to tag the leader. If the leader catches the ball before anyone tags him or her, the other students have to freeze and start over. Whoever manages to tag the leader before the ball is caught becomes the leader.

Quarterback Rescue *(from physical education teacher Mark Farnsworth)*

This game is played with two teams in a playing area that has a center line and end lines to mark each team's end zone. Divide each team in half. One half of the team stays in their own playing area; the other half moves to the opposing team's end zone. The goal of the game is for each team to rescue team members from the opposing end zone by throwing them a ball. The players in the end zone must catch the ball in the air and throw a completed pass back to a teammate. When they've done this, they can join their teammates in the playing area and attempt to rescue others from the end zone. To de-emphasize competition, stop the game before all players are rescued.

Everybody Kicks Kickball *(from fourth grade teacher Andy Dousis)*

This game is played with similar rules to traditional kickball but there are no teams and students rotate through positions. Set up the playing area as you would for traditional kickball. The pitcher rolls the ball towards home plate, the kicker kicks

the ball, and attempts to run the bases before a fielder catches the ball and tags the base. Begin by assigning numbers to each position; some teachers use the traditional baseball numbering system where the pitcher is number one, the catcher is number two, followed in order by first, second, and third base, shortstop, and left, center, and right field. Students who are not in the field line up to kick the ball. As soon as a kicker is out, everyone rotates: Position number one moves to number two and so on. Position number nine moves to the end of the line waiting to kick the ball.

Blanketball (from physical education teacher Mark Farnsworth)

Divide the class into two teams. Each team spreads out around its own sturdy blanket or sheet. Team members grasp the edges of the blanket and a ball is placed in the middle of the cloth. Each group practices tossing the ball into the air and catching it with the cloth. Teams then pass one ball back and forth. Alternatively, one team can toss a ball straight up, quickly get out of the way, and let the other team rush in to catch the ball with their cloth.

Silly Soccer (from Greenfield Center School staff)

As in traditional soccer, competing teams try to score a goal by kicking a ball. However, in Silly Soccer, there are three goals and no traditional soccer rules. Arrange the playing field in a triangle with a cone at each point of the triangle. The cones serve as the goals. Divide the class into three teams, each of which defends one of the cones, without the use of a goalie. All at the same time, the teams try to kick the ball into the other two teams' cones. Most players will give up on trying to keep track of a score and will simply have fun. A ball that's lopsided and rolls in unpredictable ways makes the game even more fun.

Fourth grade teacher Andy Dousis is a firm believer in finding alternatives to competition on the playground. But he notes ruefully that some children, boys in particular, have a hard time adjusting to the idea of cooperative play. "Many of them just want to win, they want finality," he says. "Sometimes there are children who might just never appreciate cooperative play."

While there will always be some children who resist the idea of playing cooperative games, the majority of girls and boys will enjoy themselves so thoroughly that they won't notice that the scoreboard has been turned off or care who is laughing and catching and throwing by their side. Educator Chip Wood feels that cooperative games also have a lasting effect:

Teaching kids how to play cooperatively and learning how to use competition without leaving people behind—these skills are going to have an enormous impact on people's adult lives, in addition to affecting how boys and girls treat each other in school.

Use simple methods for forming inclusive teams

"Okay, everybody!" shouts Mr. Everett, as the third graders tumble out the gym doors and gather around to pick teams for kickball. "Captains: Joey and Simon! Simon gets first picks because Blue team lost yesterday. Let's go!"

This is the beginning of a common scenario, with a predictable outcome. Joey and Simon will choose their teams based in part on friendships and in part on perceived athletic ability. Inevitably someone's feelings will be hurt. Let's see how this scenario ends:

Simon surveys the line of remaining children, all girls except for Ben and Elliott. Reluctantly, he chooses: "Ben." Joey picks Elliott. The choosing of girls is accomplished without pause or thought until only Maggie and Olivia are left.

Joey and Simon pause again, looking back and forth between the two girls, clearly not wanting to pick either one. Joey sighs. "Maggie." The two teams noisily run for the kickball diamond, the boys on Joey's team scrambling for the bases, while the girls wander into the outfield. Olivia's name is never called.

Team-picking scenarios such as these are public acts of choosing that assign every child a place in the class hierarchy of athletic ability and popularity. Every child is aware of who is wanted, who is merely tolerated, and who is actively unwanted.

The best way to avoid these scenarios is by playing cooperative games where there are no teams. When you do play team-based games, here are three simple ways to form teams that are inclusive and promote positive relationships among the students:

Have students count off and gather according to number.

If you sense that students are organizing themselves so that they end up on a team with their best friends, you could have them first line up by height, birth date, alphabet, or another arbitrary system. Then they can count off by twos or threes and gather according to number.

Put slips of paper with colored dots (or stickers or shapes) into a basket.

Children draw a slip of paper and then gather with other children who have the same color dot, animal, shape, etc.

The teacher assigns teams ahead.

If balancing skill levels is important, then the teacher should take the responsibility for making team assignments ahead of time, based on her/his knowledge of the students.

Sometimes it's important for team members to easily identify each other, as in Capture the Flag. It's tempting in that case to divide the group according to gender. However, this works against building good cross-gender relationships on the playground. Instead, you could make sashes or arm bands out of two different colors of crepe paper.

When recess is carefully structured and games are cooperative and inclusive, there are many opportunities for boys and girls to play alongside one another and fewer chances that children will feel left out. In this climate, it is also less likely that children will be teased for playing on the opposite side of the gender line. In fact, eventually the gender line will become so insignificant that children will not even know where it stands. As an added bonus, structured play reduces tension and aggression on the playground, which means that less time is spent in the classroom dealing with the problems that arise during recess and more time is available for learning.

Works Cited

Orlick, Terry. 1978. *The Cooperative Sports & Games Book: Challenge Without Competition*. New York, NY: Pantheon Books.

Thorne, Barrie. 1993. *Gender Play: Girls and Boys in School*. New Brunswick, NJ: Rutgers University Press.

Conclusion

Creating a Place Where Children Can Care about Each Other

T HE TENDENCY OF CHILDREN to divide by gender is only one of the challenges that teachers face when they attempt to build community in the classroom and the school. But it is a substantial challenge! If we want children to learn how to get along with, appreciate, and care for each other, in spite of differences, what better place to start than with the other half of the population? And what better time to start than in the first days of school?

Habit is an amazing, powerful force. Students who each day line up, talk, work, and play with both boys and girls grow comfortable with gender mixing. Students who learn about both women's and men's achievements are more likely to feel confidence in their own potential and respectful of each other's striving to make a place in the world. Students who each day question the status quo find it much easier to continue questioning, even when the status quo involves something as ancient, tangled, and deeply-entrenched as gender roles and relationships.

This is not to say that it always comes easily or naturally. We teachers—women and men who are as steeped in societal norms as our students—find ourselves constantly moving along a continuum of attitudes. From year to year, class to class, experience to experience, our learning curve remains high. One veteran teacher describes an event that surprised and enlightened the staff at her school. They had recently completed in-service work to raise gender awareness and improve gender relations in the school:

> We were doing a production of *Cinderella*, and after weeks of practicing and building and getting ready, the show went on. Then suddenly, from backstage, some of us realized: *Oh, no! What have we done? He's marrying her just because she's*

beautiful, and she's marrying him just because he's the prince! They don't know anything about each other! They've only met one time! What kind of message are we sending?

My desire in writing this book is to give teachers safe, positive, proactive ways to bring girls and boys together in their classrooms. My hope is that teachers will benefit from the wealth of enabling suggestions and take heart from the unanimous agreement of all the teachers interviewed for these pages:

1. It's well worth the time and effort to teach and model good gender relations from kindergarten on up.

2. Progress may seem slow, but it does come, in increments, over time.

The seeds you plant with first graders may not take root for several years, but by helping children learn to value and respect each other, you are making a positive impact on their lives.

Finally, I hope this book gives teachers courage to call on the authority of the school and on their own authority in the classroom to create a more rewarding gender climate for everyone. "In our school," this authority asserts, "we are friendly to everybody. There's a place for everybody." Such a school or classroom provides many opportunities to genuinely, safely, and openly care about each other, regardless of gender.

Resources

(*Cited as a reference.)

Introduction: Girls on One Side, Boys on the Other

Jossey-Bass Publishers. 2002. *The Jossey-Bass Reader on Gender in Education*. San Francisco: Jossey-Bass.

A comprehensive anthology that explores the range of opinions and approaches to the topic of gender equity in education.

Thorne, Barrie. 1993. *Gender Play: Girls and Boys in School*. New Brunswick, NJ: Rutgers University Press.*

Sociologist Barrie Thorne observes children in upper elementary classrooms and schools and discusses the ways that social context influences children's experience of gender.

Teacher Awareness: The Starting Point

Horgan, Dianne D. 1995. *Achieving Gender Equity: Strategies for the Classroom*. Boston: Allyn and Bacon.*

Includes a detailed "gender audit" that helps teachers take a close look at classroom management decisions.

Wood, Chip. 1997. *Yardsticks: Children in the Classroom Ages 4-14, A Resource for Parents and Teachers*. Greenfield, MA: Northeast Foundation for Children.*

Clear and concise descriptions of children's developmental stages. Includes charts that summarize physical, social, language, and cognitive growth for each age group as well as points on applying the information to curricular areas.

Classroom Management

Brady, Kathryn, Mary Beth Forton, Deborah Porter, and Chip Wood. 2003. *Rules in School.* Greenfield, MA: Northeast Foundation for Children.*

Presents a positive approach to helping students become invested in creating and living by classroom rules.

Charney, Ruth Sidney. 2002. *Teaching Children to Care: Classroom Management for Ethical and Academic Growth, K–8.* Greenfield, MA: Northeast Foundation for Children.

Shows teachers how to turn their vision of respectful, friendly, academically rigorous classrooms into reality.

Denton, Paula, and Roxann Kriete. 2000. *The First Six Weeks of School.* Greenfield, MA: Northeast Foundation for Children.*

Shows teachers how to use the first six weeks of school to lay the groundwork for a productive year of learning.

Developmental Studies Center. 1997. *Blueprints for a Collaborative Classroom.* Oakland, CA: Developmental Studies Center.

Provides ideas for teaching students how to collaborate throughout the school day. Includes twenty-five designs for partner and group work.

_____. 1996. *Ways We Want Our Class to Be: Class Meetings That Build Commitment to Kindness and Learning.* Oakland, CA: Developmental Studies Center.

Includes information on why, when, and how to use class meetings; strategies for various kinds of meetings; and examples of meetings in action.

Faber, Adele, and Elaine Mazlish. 1995. *How to Talk So Kids Can Learn at Home and in School.* New York, NY: Simon and Schuster.

Shows teachers how to use a "dialogue" technique and handle behavioral and peer problems that can interfere with learning.

Froschl, Merle, Barbara Sprung, and Nancy Mullin-Rindler with Nan Stein and Nancy Gropper. 1998. *Quit It! A Teacher's Guide on Teasing and Bullying for Use with Students in Grades K-3.* New York, NY: Educational Equity Concepts; Wellesley, MA: Wellesley College Center for Research on Women.

> In workbook format, presents a series of lessons to help children address and prevent teasing and bullying. Themes include creating rules, talking about teasing and bullying, and exploring how to do the right thing. Also includes games, calming exercises, and problem-solving techniques. Available through Wellesley Centers for Women (www.wcwonline.org).

Kriete, Roxann. 2002. *The Morning Meeting Book.* Greenfield, MA: Northeast Foundation for Children.*

> Gives an in-depth description of, and guidelines for using, Morning Meetings in K–8 classrooms.

Nelsen, Jane, Lynn Lott, and H. Stephen Glenn. 2000. *Positive Discipline in the Classroom: Developing Mutual Respect, Cooperation, and Responsibility in Your Classroom.* Roseville, CA: Prima Publishing.

> Includes comprehensive information about using problem-solving class meetings at various grade levels.

Sapon-Shevin, Mara. 1999. *Because We Can Change the World: A Practical Guide to Building Cooperative, Inclusive Classroom Communities.* Boston, MA: Allyn and Bacon.

> Provides many practical ideas for building community in the classroom. Each chapter includes activities, games, songs, books for children to read, and links to the curriculum.

Sjostrom, Lisa, and Nan Stein. 1996. *Bullyproof: A Teacher's Guide on Teasing and Bullying for Use with Fourth and Fifth Grade Students.* Wellesley, MA: Wellesley College Center for Research on Women; Washington, DC: NEA Professional Library.

> Includes eleven core lessons, some of which take several class sessions. Students learn to differentiate between teasing and bullying and intervene when they see bullying occur. Available through Wellesley Centers for Women (www.wcwonline.org).

Teaching Tolerance Project. 1997. *Starting Small: Teaching Tolerance in Preschool and the Early Grades.* Montgomery, AL: Southern Poverty Law Center.

Includes profiles from classrooms around the country, reflection on the issues, and practical strategies for teaching tolerance.

The Curriculum

Carlsson-Paige, Nancy, and Diane E. Levin. 1990. *Who's Calling the Shots? How to Respond Effectively to Children's Fascination with War Play and War Toys and Violent TV!* Gabriola Island, BC: New Society Publishers.*

Gives practical suggestions for encouraging young children's imaginative, dramatic play.

Clayton, Marlynn K., with Mary Beth Forton. 2001. *Classroom Spaces That Work.* Greenfield, MA: Northeast Foundation for Children.

Helps teachers create a physical environment that is developmentally appropriate, organized, and welcoming.

Cooney, Miriam P. ed. 1997. *Celebrating Women in Mathematics and Science.* Reston, VA: National Council of Teachers of Mathematics.

Features twenty-two biographies of notable female mathematicians and scientists, from Hypatia to Maria Gaetana Agnesi, Sophie Germain, Caroline Herschel, Grace Hopper (the computer pioneer and admiral), and many more.

Council on Interracial Books for Children. "10 Quick Ways to Analyze Children's Books for Racism and Sexism." Adapted from *Guidelines for Selecting Bias-Free Textbooks and Storybooks.* 1980. New York, NY: The Council.

The text of this pamphlet is available online from http://www.birchlane.davis.ca.us/library/10quick.htm. The ten strategies can help teachers do a comprehensive review of texts and literature.

Hurst, Carol Otis, and Rebecca Hurst. 1999. *Friends and Relations: Using Literature with Social Themes K-2.* Greenfield, MA: Northeast Foundation for Children.

—————————————————————. *2000. Friends and Relations: Using Literature with Social Themes Grades 3 -5.* Greenfield, MA: Northeast Foundation for Children.

Both books offer information about children's books that explore social interests central to children's lives. Thematic issues include friendship; bullies, pests, and teasing; and families. Both books include content summaries, suggested discussion questions, and suggested activities based on the books.

McGowan, Meredith, Tom McGowan, and Pat Wheeler. 1994. *Appreciating Diversity Through Children's Literature: Teaching Activities for the Primary Grades.* Englewood, CO: Teacher Ideas Press.

Looks at four diversity themes: age, gender, physical ability, and ethnicity. In each section, the authors consider several titles. They provide a summary of each book and present a wide range of classroom activities.

Rudman, Masha. 1995. *Children's Literature: An Issues Approach.* 3rd edition. White Plains, NY: Longman Publishers.*

First published in 1976, this book was updated and expanded for its third edition. Divided into three thematic units—family, life cycle, and society—the book presents detailed, in-depth information about using literature to help children explore such issues as siblings, divorce, aging, gender roles, and heritage. Each chapter includes a comprehensive resource list and bibliography.

Sprung, Barbara. 1975. *Non-Sexist Education for Young Children.* New York, NY: Educational Equity Concepts.

Curriculum guide to practical, easy-to-use approaches to bias-free early education.

Sprung, Barbara, Merle Froschl, and Patricia B. Campbell. 1985. *What Will Happen If...Young Children and the Scientific*

Method. New York, NY: Educational Equity Concepts.

An equity-based early physical science curriculum.

Trentacosta, Janet ed. 1997. *Multicultural and Gender Equity in the Mathematics Classroom: The Gift of Diversity* (1997 Yearbook). Reston, VA: National Council of Teachers of Mathematics.

Contains numerous ideas for providing K–12 mathematics programs for students of any race, ethnicity, language, gender, or socioeconomic situation.

Vare, Ethlie Ann, and Greg Ptacek. 1988. *Mothers of Invention: From the Bra to the Bomb: Forgotten Women and Their Unforgettable Ideas.* New York, NY: William Morrow and Company.

Contains over one hundred brief biographies of women inventors.

Outside the Classroom

Clements, Rhonda L., ed. 2000. *Elementary School Recess: Selected Readings, Games, and Activities for Teachers and Parents.* Boston, MA: American Press.

Makes the case for elementary school recess and offers articles on how to make recess successful. Includes a collection of classic games.

Gregson, Bob. 1984. *The Outrageous Outdoor Games Book.* Illustrated by the author. Torrance, CA: Fearon Teacher Aids.

Presents 133 projects, games, and activities that require minimal preparation and planning, and invite group interaction.

Harrison, Adrian. 2002. *36 Games Kids Love to Play.* Illustrated by the author. Greenfield, MA: Northeast Foundation for Children.

Presents thirty-six games for grades K–4. Games are designed to maximize fun and challenge, and minimize the risk of emotional and physical harm. Collection includes adaptations of traditional favorites and new creations. All games are easy to teach and learn.

Luvmour, Sambhava, and Josette Luvmour. 1990. *Everyone Wins! Cooperative Games and Activities.* Illustrated by Susan Hill. Gabriola Island, BC; Stony Creek, CT: New Society Publishers.

Presents over 150 cooperative games and activities designed to help children resolve conflict, enhance communication, build self-esteem, and have fun.

Orlick, Terry. 1978. *The Cooperative Sports & Games Book: Challenge Without Competition.* New York, NY: Pantheon Books.*

_____. 1982. *The Second Cooperative Sports & Games Book: Over Two Hundred Noncompetitive Games for Kids and Adults Both.* New York, NY: Pantheon Books.

Together, these books present over 300 old and new games that are based on cooperation, not competition. The emphasis is on imagination rather than expensive equipment.

About the Author

Tamara Grogan has taught French and English for seventeen years at every grade level from kindergarten through continuing education. Her stories and essays have appeared in several literary journals, and she has written articles for *Responsive Classroom: A Newsletter and Resource Catalog,* and the *Responsive Classroom* website, www.responsiveclassroom.org.

The Responsive Classroom® Approach

Many of the teachers interviewed for this book use the *Responsive Classroom* approach to teaching and learning. Developed by classroom teachers, this approach consists of practical strategies for bringing together social and academic learning throughout the school day.

Guiding Principles

The *Responsive Classroom* approach is based on developmental and social learning theory and informed by years of experience in the classroom. There are seven basic principles underlying this approach:

1. The social curriculum is as important as the academic curriculum.

2. How children learn is as important as what children learn: process and content go hand-in-hand.

3. The greatest cognitive growth occurs through social interaction.

4. There is a specific set of social skills that children need to learn and practice in order to be successful academically and socially: cooperation, assertion, responsibility, empathy, and self-control (CARES).

5. Knowing the children we teach—individually, culturally, and developmentally—is as important as knowing the content we teach.

6. Knowing the families of the children we teach and encouraging their participation is as important as knowing the children we teach.

7. How we, the adults at school, work together is as important as our individual competence: lasting change begins with the adult community.

Six Strategies

The principles of the *Responsive Classroom* approach are supported by six teaching strategies:

- Morning Meeting: A daily routine that builds community, creates a positive climate for learning, and reinforces academic and social skills

- Rules and Logical Consequences: A clear and consistent approach to discipline that fosters responsibility and self-control

- Guided Discovery: A format for introducing materials that encourages inquiry, heightens interest, and teaches care of the school environment

- Academic Choice: An approach to giving children choices in their learning in order to help them become invested, self-motivated learners

- Classroom Organization: Strategies for arranging materials, furniture, and displays to encourage independence, promote caring, and maximize learning

- Communicating with Families: Ideas for involving families as true partners in their children's education

**For more information about
the *Responsive Classroom* approach,
please contact us at:**

Responsive Classroom®

NORTHEAST FOUNDATION FOR CHILDREN
39 Montague City Road, Greenfield, MA 01301
Phone 800-360-6332 or 413-772-2066 Fax 413-774-1129

www.responsiveclassroom.org

Other Titles in the Small Book Series
from Northeast Foundation for Children

#1

Off to a Good Start: Launching the School Year
Excerpts from the Responsive Classroom Newsletter
For K–6 teachers (1997) 66 pages

Includes nine of the most frequently requested *Responsive Classroom* newsletter articles that feature ideas for building a strong and caring learning community.

#2

Familiar Ground:
Traditions that Build School Community
by Libby Woodfin
For K–8 teachers (1998) 72 pages

See how Greenfield Center School, the independent school founded by Northeast Foundation for Children, uses traditions to create a strong sense of whole-school community. Includes both descriptions of the traditions and guidelines for implementing them.

#3

Friends and Relations:
Using Literature with Social Themes K–2
by Carol Otis Hurst and Rebecca Otis
For K–2 teachers (1999) 108 pages

Recommendations for fifteen great books that explore social themes with kindergartners through second graders. Topics include friendship, bullying, and families. Gives group activities as well as questions and topics for prompting good discussions.

#4

Friends and Relations:
Using Literature with Social Themes Grades 3-5
by Carol Otis Hurst and Rebecca Otis
For grade 3–5 teachers (2000) 90 pages

Recommendations for eight great books for the upper elementary grades. Focuses on themes of friendship and family. Includes activities to enhance understanding, suggestions and techniques for facilitating in-depth discussions, and an annotated list of thematically related books.

For a free newsletter/catalog
of resources or to order a book,
please contact us at:

NORTHEAST FOUNDATION FOR CHILDREN
39 Montague City Road, Greenfield, MA 01301
Phone 800-360-6332 or 413-772-2066 Fax 413-774-1129

www.responsiveclassroom.org